L
K.

# Whiddin to the Gauras

## Talking to Our Own

# to the Gauras

# Whiddin to the Gauras

## Talking to Our Own

# Traveller Researchers talk to Limerick Traveller Children

Researchers: Mags Casey,
Ann O'Donoghue, Bridgie O'Donoghue,
Ann O'Driscoll

Written and compiled by
Eleanor Gormally

**VERITAS**

*First published 2005 by*
Veritas Publications
7/8 Lower Abbey Street
Dublin 1
Ireland
Email publications@veritas.ie
Website www.veritas.ie

ISBN 1 85390 863 0

The photographs in this book represent Traveller children in
general; they are not photographs of the children interviewed.

Designed by Colette Dower
Printed in the Republic of Ireland by Betaprint, Dublin

*Veritas books are printed on paper made from the wood pulp of
managed forests. For every tree felled, at least one tree is planted,
thereby renewing natural resources.*

*Dedicated to the memory of*
*Patrick Harty*
*Aged 9*

# Contents

# Acknowledgements

The authors wish to gratefully acknowledge the financial support received from Mary Immaculate College Research Directorate which contributed significantly to compiling the research data reported in this publication. We thank Mary Immaculate College for facilitating the research and for the help and advice received from a wide range of people within the college. Their help was invaluable.

We acknowledge the financial support received from ZONTA International through the National Women's Council of Ireland. We are grateful for their guidance and support during the course of the project and for extending our funding for a second period.

We wish to thank Limerick Travellers Development Group for their constant interest in our work.

Finally we wish to give a special note of thanks to Helen Whelehan for her wonderful encouragement and belief in the project.

# Preface

*Whiddin to the Gauras – Talking to Our Own* is a fascinating account of a unique and innovative research project involving Traveller researchers. The book outlines how four Traveller women designed a qualitative study, talked to Limerick Traveller children about their education experiences, and presented their findings in a manner that honours the voice of the young Traveller. Throughout the research programme the project leader offered strong and consistent support to the Traveller researchers. Decisions were made democratically indicating a way of working that comes across as genuinely engaging with the spirit of intercultural dialogue and respect. The study offers the reader insights into the imaginings of a group of Limerick Traveller children and an understanding of how they perceive their education and life experience, their hopes and aspirations.

I commend *Whiddin to the Gauras* to you not only because of the research findings but also for the manner in which the initiative was conducted. The unfolding process described in the study involving intercultural education and ongoing training for the Traveller researchers underlines the importance of the 'how' as well as the 'what' of the programme. The account is a clear indication that working with people as subjects rather than as objects can be a legitimate and successful part of a research process. Moreover given that not only the Traveller children, but also the Traveller researchers have experienced (and continue to experience) inequalities in education the study confirms the reality that those experiencing the issues have an incontestable right to investigate and evaluate them.

The publication is divided into three parts clearly reflecting the overall philosophy and approach of the study – an organic process based on dialogue and debate and the value of all involved moving together towards the achievement of an agreed task. Working to secure and maintain respectful relations was central. The evolving dynamic served to enrich both the process and outcome.

Part One focuses on what the Traveller researchers had to say about their experience of participating in the project. From the women themselves we learn about the importance of ongoing support and education for the development of self-confidence. We are also given significant insights into the relations between Traveller adults and Traveller children. The depth of this relationship is evidenced in the impact that the death of the child to whom the book is dedicated had on the research team. It is also a reminder of the reality of untimely death in Travellers' lives.

Based on a starting point that acknowledges the importance of education, the complex relationship between Travellers and the education system and the extent of Travellers' educational inequality, Part Two focuses on the 'who', the 'what', the 'when', the 'where' and the 'how' of the research. The process, consultation and design is described in detail and in a way that is useful both for this study and for replication by others. Issues that emerged during both the development and implementation phases are discussed. These include an account of the overall positive reception received by the Traveller researchers when conducting the interviews in the schools.

Part Three of *Whiddin to the Gauras* tells us what the children said. The commentary on what the children recount makes for very interesting reading, for as well as presenting the insights in readable manner it gives us a clear indication of the group's concerns and respect for their interviewees and their issues. The detail of the discussions provides us with food for thought and further analysis.

This is a qualitative study, therefore the sample is small. However there is no doubt that the experiences outlined and the conclusions drawn will resonate for Travellers and Traveller organisations well beyond the environs of Limerick city and the surrounding area. From my own work with Travellers in Ireland over the past twenty years I am conscious of many such resonances – the importance of Traveller symbols and images in classrooms and of the ways in which Traveller self-confidence and self-identity can be eroded through ongoing negative experiences and perceptions. I am conscious also from my work in Europe of resonances with the experiences of the Roma, Sinti and Travellers throughout Europe and beyond. Education may be crucial. However it is becoming increasingly evident that successful educational outcomes are not automatic even where enrolment and/or attendance are no longer the primary issues.

The publication of *Whiddin to the Gauras* is particularly timely as deliberations on the National Traveller Education Strategy draw to a close. The strategy, which is one of the outcomes of the 1995 Task Force on Travellers will chart policy, objectives and targets for Traveller education into the foreseeable future. As this research indicates, and as Roma, Sinti and Traveller groups across Europe can endorse, a key to success will be the acknowledgement and respect for Traveller identity. Identity denial, one of the most common forms of discrimination against Travellers everywhere has no part in good education practice and can only lead to a continuation of negative outcomes. The conclusion and recommendations emphasise the importance of the Traveller researchers taking up a key role in their implementation. This is very much in line with the spirit of the entire study. The recommendations contain proposals worthy of future consideration by statutory bodies, local authorities and Traveller organisations at all levels.

The perspective of this endeavour is clearly that of the Traveller. There are many other perspectives, including those of education providers and professionals, which may or may not concur with the totality of what is written. Nonetheless I believe there is considerable learning to be gained for all in the experiences and issues so meticulously described – whatever the perspective. I urge the reader towards the place where the messages can be heard or acted on.

I take this opportunity to congratulate all involved – researchers, programme leader and young participants – and to wish them well with their work, education and lives. I am sure the experience was challenging and at times frustrating, but all remained steadfast and committed to the end.

I hope you have found enrichment in your achievement. I hope your efforts will be rewarded and acknowledged ultimately through a future of respect and equality for Travellers everywhere.

Anastasia Crickley
Lecturer in Applied Social Studies – NUI Maynooth
Chairperson of the NCCRI (National Consultative Committee
on Racism and Interculturalism)
Chairperson of the EUMC (European Union Monitoring
Committee on Racism and Xenophobia)

# Introduction

In 2001 a research-training project was undertaken jointly by Mary Immaculate College of Education and Limerick Travellers Development Group. Mary Immaculate, Limerick is a leading provider in the field of third-level education. Limerick Travellers Development Group, the local Traveller Community Development Project plays a central and significant role in the demand for Traveller rights, at local and national levels. Both organisations share a common vision – namely the desire to work towards the promotion of a just society where diversity is respected and equality is the right of all. Their mission statements reflect this aspiration.

Limerick Travellers Development Group seeks: 'To work towards a partnership of Travellers and members of the majority population, based on a respect for Traveller culture with the aim of promoting Traveller rights, dignity and equality.'

Mary Immaculate College of Education: 'respects cultural diversity. It strives to promote equity in society and to provide an environment where all have freedom and opportunity to achieve their full potential.'

This cross-sector initiative between Limerick Travellers Development Group and Mary Immaculate College set out to create a context where members of the Traveller community would be trained in basic qualitative research skills and in the application of those skills through a series of interviews with a group of Limerick Traveller children. A collaborative-partnership model of training was adopted. This model built on the diversity within the group and ensured that the training was participant led at all times. The diversity within the group was reflected in the personal histories echoed in particular experiences of social privilege or social disadvantage, of Traveller or settled, of educational exclusion or inclusion, of work perspectives and world-views. An intricate interweaving of these rich threads shaped the 'tapestry' of this partnership. Identifying and accepting difference as both positive and valuable was foundational to the entire undertaking.

The project developed organically through dialogue, debate and consensus. However, three fundamental principles guided the proceedings from the onset. They were as follows:

1. that the partnership and diversity between the parties be honoured and safeguarded (relationship).
2. that the manner in which the team worked be valued and be appraised regularly through participant review and evaluation (process).
3. that the group move towards the accomplishment of the agreed task (result).

These three dimensions of relationship, process and result are fundamental to the success of any project. Frequently, success is measured in terms of result and outcome alone. Doing so can diminish the importance of the two other essential elements – *how* the task is achieved (process) and *how* people relate to one another during the completion of the task (relationship). When results alone become the focus, the relationship and process may become a mere means to an end and are often not fully recognised as valid aspects in the success of a project. For those of us working within 'academia', measurement by result has a familiar ring. For those of us who work from a community development perspective, the process and the relationship are viewed as vital elements to be respected when working towards a desired outcome.

This initiative attempted to hold the tension between the three elements – relationship, process and result. It sought to do so in a way that offered equal attention to participant relationship, to the management of the study and to the final outcomes. This entailed agreeing clear goals for completion, regularly reviewing how the tasks were performed through participant evaluation and maximising the engagement of each member of the group by preserving a positive climate of mutual learning. Trust was a key and sustaining factor. Establishing a trusting partnership in a group that reflected cultural, educational and institutional diversity demanded high levels of respect, openness and honesty. Time and again trust was built through the testimony of personal experiences and life stories. The recounting of individual histories and cultural diversity defined the partnership and led to insights and discoveries that proved to be transforming.

An environment of acceptance where genuine and sincere dialogue took place grew gradually. As the group evolved in confidence and people became more at ease with one another the sharing took on a critical edge that provoked much analysis at personal and systemic levels. Views became challenged, perceptions questioned, language translated, systems critiqued, stereotyping confronted and throughout it all friendships were formed.

What is presented in the following pages is the result of a very rich and often complex process. Part 1 offers a direct insight into the Traveller researchers' experience of participating in the project. Part 2 outlines the steps of the process and describes the method of study and its design. Part 3 presents the data commentary and interpretation. Extracts from the children's interviews are offered allowing the reader access to the voices of Traveller children. Selecting material for inclusion in a document of this nature is never neutral. However the extracts are typical of what the children said on a given topic. They are not meant to be viewed in a quantitative fashion. They are merely a sample of the sort of information the children offered when chatting about their experiences. In the interest of honouring confidentiality and preserving identity cross referencing between individual interviews has not been included.

It is our hope that in outlining the process of the initiative encouragement might be given to other Traveller Community Development Groups to initiate or participate in similar kinds of partnership research.

# Part 1
# What the Women Said

*What the Traveller researchers had to say*
*about their experience of participating*
*in the project*

**The Project**

'When I started doing this piece of research or when I was asked if I'd be interested in doing it I said, "I won't be able to do this!"'

'I think when we started we did not think that it would take so much time. But now we are nearly finished I have done so much. Now it is hard to believe that we have gone so far with this work.'

'When we first started this research I took it on board to get out of the house to meet the girls. I didn't realise the amount of work that was going to go into the project. I would never have thought that it would need that much work and time. But as we got going I felt that this was my way of showing what I, as a Traveller woman with little education, could do.'

'It was a big commitment, bigger than I expected. I thought that it would be just a couple of meetings here and there. I didn't realise that we would have been so committed to it. There would have been nights when I was wondering if I should have stayed at home with a sick child. Then other nights I would be delighted to get out of the home for a break away from the hassles. Concentrating on what was going on at the meeting I would forget what was happening at home!'

'When issues came up at home it was difficult at times. But I made time for it because I was interested in it and I wanted to do it.'

'The times of meetings didn't always suit everybody. College, childcare, home; juggling the time to fit all in was really hard for me.'

'It has been a struggle to us all juggling homes, families, college. Child care was a constant issue, but I fitted the research in because I wanted to do the research and I enjoyed it so much.'

'At the end we will have something back. But at the beginning I asked myself did this amount of work need to go into it? But working as hard as we did was the only way if we wanted to get something back in return.'

'Sometimes because it was taking so long I was hoping that it would be finished soon. Yet now when it is coming to an end I don't want it to finish. It's a bit like retiring from the job!'

**The Working Group**
'We worked very well together as a group. We recognised what skills people had. The meetings were very good. Often the meetings were like counselling and we sometimes came out for this reason. I feel very close to the group because of the research.'

'It has been great working with the group. We have learnt so much from each other.'

'We were conscious of challenging each other. I think that from the first day we began I was looking for evidence of discrimination. Because I, as a Traveller, experienced discrimination in the education system and I know that it is still there in many different forms.'

'The group had to be patient with me. I felt supported by the group. I wouldn't have gone as far as I did without the support of the group. When any of us was down we pulled each other up together; that was the way the group worked! We all pulled one another along.'

'I have had other experiences of working in and with groups in the past. I feel this was a very positive experience for me. I felt our group gelled and bonded very well and that a lot of work was done in a safe atmosphere.'

'We all had other commitments and we understood that, but there were other occasions when we didn't understand the commitments of other members of the group. But as we gelled we understood more about each other and if someone wasn't at a meeting we knew why. We worked well together, I thought.'

'Even though we worked hard we always had time for a chit-chat and a lot of important stuff came up in these little chit-chats. Sometimes it was even personal stuff that a member of the group wanted to get off her chest and if she was willing to talk about it, it always helped to thrash things out in the group.'

'We learnt a lot from working together. We learnt about other people and relationships. The work together opened up a different side to other people, a more sensitive side.'

'I also felt the group had a lot to cope with. Most of us come from the same worker-mother background, but we were all different. As a group we had great patience with each other, especially around attendance, things that weren't easy because we all had issues like childcare, timekeeping, sickness. Some of us were completing college diplomas and needed the support and patience of the group.'

'I feel that we have been through a lot as a group in the past three years! We are better individuals for working as members of the research project.'

'We got on well as a group. I saw us all growing as we went along.'

**The Research**
'It was interesting going to the sites and getting permission from the parents of Traveller children and explaining the whole thing to them.'

'Analysing the data and working with the AnnoTape (computer program) for the themes was a huge challenge and a huge learning. I benefited from it. It made me more confident in dealing with that kind of research material. I can now do that sort of thing in my present job.'

'I enjoyed analysing the interviews.'

'For me it wasn't always easy to agree with the others about the interpretation – what or where the children were coming from. There might be difference in relation to understanding the Traveller culture or understanding discrimination and I'd say "This is what the children are saying". At times we didn't always agree. It was interesting how different people see stuff differently.'

'We had our meetings in the college. We learnt to use Mary Immaculate College.'

'I feel very proud of myself that I could go to the computer by myself and get into and use AnnoTape. It was a great achievement for me as a mother.'

'In the interviews with the children we stuck to the questions we had agreed on as a group. I felt that we might have done better if we hadn't stuck to the questions so much. Listening back we could see what it was we could have asked. If I hadn't been so aware of leading questions I would have done a better interview out of the children. If I was doing it again I would just have a set of guideline questions, but not set questions, and I would let the children wander more.'

'Using the machines during the interviews was another big challenge. I felt that we were not fully relaxed interviewing the children because of the machines. We kept wondering, "is it working?" Anyone doing research shouldn't have that pressure. We would have relaxed more if it was better set up.'

'The machines distracted the children. The children were very curious about them. Maybe we could find easier machines to use, less obvious machines if we were doing it again.'

'If we were to do it again we would give more time to getting used to the equipment – mini-disc and Dictaphone machines – before going to the schools. We had never used these machines before. We should have concentrated on them more, that's what I would do if I was to do the research again.'

'I was very confident going into the schools. I was confident as a Traveller. I felt that we could do it. I felt that we could be professional. We were there to do the research. We didn't want the schools to see us as the "typical" Traveller.'

'I enjoyed challenging the teachers about Traveller education. Having had a difficult time in school myself I could relate to the discrimination that the children were facing. But I was able to challenge the teachers about discrimination. I challenged one teacher in relation to Traveller culture and the equal education for Travellers. She had her own views of Travellers and where they fitted in. I felt that I was able to challenge her and tell her that perhaps it was her attitude that should change, and not the Travellers.'

'It was a big challenge for me to walk into schools for the interviews. I was very nervous when meeting with the teachers. I felt we had a very pleasant experience in the main school I was interviewing in. But some staff in another school was rude to us and that was an issue for us to deal with.'

'I felt professional going to the school because of the training we had beforehand.'

'I felt that some schools treated us disrespectfully. One school in particular treated us really well. We knew immediately that we were welcome in this school. In this particular school we were encouraged and questioned in a nice way. The staff was not suspicious of us. They would always dedicate a room for us with no interruptions. They went out of their way to make us welcome. They trusted us as individuals.'

'How the teachers behaved with us was a big thing for us because we had other experiences that weren't so positive.'

'The reception from the schools was overall good, except for the one school that refused to facilitate us to do the interviews during school time. I was very disappointed about the school that wouldn't let us in as researchers. I was disappointed that we didn't do anything about it. Many Traveller children are not happy there.'

'When we went out to the schools we tried to be professional by not being rude in spite of all the interruptions from some of the teachers in some of the schools. We found that some of the teachers were inquisitive. They were asking a lot of questions about the research project. It was all new to ourselves, so giving them details of the research and being professional all at once was a challenge for us.'

'At one stage we had to make a presentation to ZEST (one of the Research Funders) and to the other project groups who had got money from ZEST. We had gone to Dublin to hear about the other projects. When the crowd came down from Dublin to us in Limerick it was good for us. They put it up to us. But we showed them what we were doing with their funding! They were very friendly people. We learnt a lot from each other.'

'We had to go to Dublin to meet up with other projects that got funding from ZEST. In going up to Dublin we saw what others were doing and that was really important. We wanted to impress them when they came down to Limerick to see what we were doing!'

### The Traveller Children
'I felt comfortable interviewing Traveller kids. I felt I could break down the questions for the kids in our own words. I thought it was fun. I enjoyed the kids.'

'I found the kids open and honest during the interviews and they had fun too.'

'I found it hard to get the kids to settle down and talk at times. Later it was easier when they started talking. It was easier also because we were Travellers.'

'In my experience of doing this research Traveller children have little or no confidence in their education. Confidence is a key thing in school and throughout life. All the Traveller children who we interviewed attended a resource teacher – how come?'

'I enjoyed the experience of interviewing the children. Lots of stuff that came from the kids I had forgotten about myself. The research reminded me about the importance of my Traveller culture.'

'I thought that the interviews with the children would have been easier. The children came out with a lot of stuff.'

'I'd know the children, as I'd be related to some of them, but I wouldn't really know them. The first thing they would ask was, "Where do you live?", "Who owns you?" When the children asked I would have to explain to them who I was. I would have to tell them before they talked, but once they knew who I was they talked away.'

'The kids would only talk if they wanted to talk, but I don't know if a settled person would get any more out of them. I think that they might fill a settled person up with a lot of rubbish and gibing because they would know that they could get away with it. They couldn't do that to us because we would know if they were telling it right or not.'

'Traveller children should be coming out of the education system with a full education, an education that lets them be able to make choices in their lives. Traditionally Travellers are blamed for not having education because of travelling or not attending school or not doing homework. So what is happening here? These are Traveller children who are attending school and some of them are not happy at school. Happiness has a lot to do with your learning.'

'The death of one of the children had a big impact on me. Of all the children I could tune into what this child was saying. He knew himself as a real Traveller. He was very confident that he was a Traveller. The other children could say it, but they weren't as conscious about being Travellers as this child was. I loved that in this child.'

'As a group we dealt with bereavement, sickness and birth over the time of the research. The death of one of the boys set us back a lot. I couldn't listen to what he said. As a mother I found it very hard and I was very sad for the child's mother too.'

**The Experience**
'It was a good experience. It felt like I was an important person going into the schools because I had the ability and the experience

to talk to the teachers and the staff. I met them on their own level.'

'As I gained more confidence in myself and had more respect for the work that we were doing, I wanted to do it right. So as I got into it I began to take it personally. I wanted the research to be as good as possible and I wanted people to be impressed with us when they met us. We were a group of Traveller women who were doing our best and we were proud of it.'

'I feel that as Traveller people there is nothing we couldn't do if people from an educated background would give us a chance. This research has made me see that there is nothing I can't do if I want to.'

'Traveller children see the world differently. It's our culture. It's our background. Because we are only a small minority our culture sticks out more. I feel, as we near the end of the research, very proud and very well able to do anything I choose. I want to pass this on to my children. I want people to see me on a professional level. I want to make an impression on others.'

'If I was to do the research again or do further research I would ask different questions. I would ask more about resource classes and what the children do in their resource classes and what they think of it and what their resource teacher is like. If I had to do it again I would ask different questions, but I only realised that from doing the research in the first place.'

'Overall I enjoyed the research!'

'I saw my children being proud of me.'

'I feel that I could stand up and say my point of view. Now I feel that if I have something to say I have enough confidence to say it as I see it. I could go to the school; meet with the teachers, speak to them on a level that I was happy with.'

'My question from this research is this: "Doesn't the education system need to change so that a community like the Traveller community can benefit from the system?"'

## The Researchers

*Mags Casey*

*Bridgie O'Donoghue*

*Ann O'Donoghue*

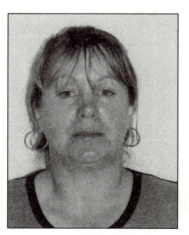

*Ann O'Driscoll*

# Part 2
# What We Did and How

## *Setting the Scene*

Travellers are one of Ireland's largest ethnic minority groups, constituting approximately 0.5 per cent of the overall population. The Irish Traveller community sees itself as a distinct group within society. A range of aspects such as its traditions, its customs, its language, the manner in which economic activity is organised and its particular belief and value system defines the uniqueness of the Traveller community as an ethnic group. A lack of understanding of and respect for Traveller culture contributes to the everyday experience of discrimination, oppression and rejection experienced by Travellers within Irish society.

Education is a key factor in the development and enhancement of Traveller participation in society. The relationship between the Traveller community and the educational system has been, and in many instances continues to be, a complicated one. Nonetheless positive developments have occurred over recent years in the provision of education for children of the Traveller community at primary level. This is acknowledged by the Irish Traveller Movement. However, while

Traveller participation at primary school level has increased substantially, the transfer to secondary school remains very low and the uptake at third level minimal.

One of the groups targeted as central to Traveller children's engagement with the education process are parents. Parental involvement in the education of children is an essential ingredient in the establishment of a successful relationship between home and school. For the majority of Traveller parents, however, participating in the provision of education to their children is a formidable task. Many Traveller parents personally feel alienated from the school system and perceive themselves as unskilled and therefore unable to support or monitor their child's educational progress. Having had limited and often negative experiences of schooling themselves they feel intimidated when crossing the threshold of the school entrance. Few structures are in place to facilitate Traveller parental engagement with the day-to-day education of their children. Those who do cross the threshold of the classroom, however, are most likely to be Traveller mothers. In Traveller culture as in most other cultures, it is the mother who typically assumes responsibility for the welfare of the family unit. Children are central to that family unit. Whatever affects the lives of Traveller children therefore directly impacts on the lives of the Traveller mother. Though the situation is changing and some Traveller fathers have increased involvement with their children, in many cases it still falls to the Traveller mother to negotiate the children's general welfare and that includes education.

**Origins of the Initiative**

In recent years a cluster of Limerick Traveller women have become increasingly aware of the importance of education in shaping the lives of their children and more and more recognise the opportunities that education can offer the next generation. They have also become acutely aware that a history of negative experiences of the education system block Traveller parents' capacity to intervene proactively in their children's education. Much of this awareness grew out of the women's involvement with the Limerick Travellers Development Group[1]. It was out of this heightened realisation that the seeds for the initiative were sown.

In September 2001 Mary Immaculate College of Education approached Limerick Travellers Development Group with a view to setting up a joint research study. Initial funding for the project was secured from Mary Immaculate College Research Directorate. Significant additional funding was accessed through ZONTA, the International ZEST Programme administered through the National Women's Council of Ireland, Dublin. The aim of the initiative was to instruct a small group of Traveller women in qualitative research skills and to support them in a fieldwork training investigation of Traveller children's experience of primary school.

The Traveller community has been researched in a variety of ways over recent years. In most cases outside 'experts' are commissioned to investigate or explore a particular aspect of Traveller culture or life. Sometimes this research is undertaken in close consultation with the Traveller community, more often it is not. The primary researcher however is typically non-Traveller. This project sought to redress this imbalance by inviting four Traveller women to collaboratively participate in, develop and implement a research training study into Traveller children. A long-term aspiration of this initiative would be that in successfully completing the training programme this group of Traveller researchers would be empowered to apply their knowledge and skills to future educational settings and so become active researchers in their own community at both local and national level.

## Outlining the Process

### Establishing the Working Group
Starting a new venture is rarely an easy matter. First steps are often taken gingerly and tentatively. The first step for this project

---

1. Limerick Travellers Development Group is a Community Development Project based in Limerick City.

was to gather together a group of interested people and to establish a formal working group. The working group comprised four local Traveller women associated with Limerick Travellers Development Group and one non-Traveller full-time member of the Department of Education, Mary Immaculate College.

The Traveller women were invited to participate in the training. They were chosen primarily because of their involvement in community development work, their association with Limerick Travellers Development Group and their long-standing interest in the educational needs of Traveller children. At the time the project was instituted two of the women were studying for a Diploma in Community Development and subsequently received their qualification in 2003. The other two women were and continue to be active members of the Limerick Travellers Development Group voluntary management committee. Each of the Traveller women had children accessing the primary school system.

The four Traveller women participated in the research training and took on the responsibility for conducting the fieldwork study. The full-time member of the Department of Education, Mary Immaculate College acted as the programme leader using the model of participative leadership. Each step of the research training programme was undertaken in complete consultation and agreement with the entire working group.

All members of the working group were fully involved in the development of the training programme and in the construction and analysis of the fieldwork study. The content of the research training programme was dictated by the specific needs of the Traveller women. The pace of the project was set by the time available to the group within an agreed time frame and by the dynamics of the work itself. Unforeseen situations, usually centering on family or work, constantly challenged the course of the programme. Evaluation and review was ongoing. This process was considered essential to the group's success and learning. The shared participant reflection was facilitated either by the programme leader or by external personnel brought in for the specific task of evaluation.

For the purpose of clarity the sequence of the process can be delineated in separate identifiable movements. I use the word 'movement' quite deliberately because it best describes the dynamic nature of the process. Movement connotes images of fluidity, change, animation, flexibility, and rhythm. If I were to describe the process in stages it might imply some sort of pre-defined or set sequence that would belie the creative energy that underpinned the working group's engagement with the project from the onset. Working with this organic, open framework brought its own particular challenges. The process was often 'messy' and demanded a high time-commitment. The 'movement' is presented below. Each aspect of the movement forms a natural coherence and succinct unit in itself. However, all aspects of the movement are inherently interconnected and are best viewed in an overarching and holistic way.

**Getting to Know One Another**
The beginning was marked by a series of introductory meetings. These sessions entailed broad, mainly unstructured discussions that focused on Traveller experience of education. They provided an opportunity for the group to chat about Traveller education and to voice areas of concern. Members of the working group knew each other prior to the development of the initiative. This impacted positively on the formation of the group in the initial stages. Despite, or perhaps because of this close familiarity the need to create and maintain a safe and accepting environment where views could be freely expressed became apparent. Preserving confidentiality within the working group became a core operational ground rule. During these sessions each member was encouraged to speak openly and freely but without coercion. Skills in active listening to, receiving and giving affirmation and constructive feedback, developing a tolerance for other viewpoints, and clear articulation of arguments were acquired during this phase. Individual members of the group shared personal experiences and named the barriers to their successful engagement in their own education and in the education of their children.

These sessions were invaluable. They served to establish the cohesion of the working group. They affirmed the power and validity of personal experience. They permitted each person to create her own identity and confidence within the group. Most significantly these meetings provided optimum conditions for the sharing of concepts, ideas, critiques and experiences of Traveller education previously unarticulated by these women in a formal Traveller/settled forum. The generative themes that emerged from these initial discussions directed the shape of the fieldwork training study.

## Consultation

Consultation was central to the working group's practice and vision. Thus early on in the proceedings the group decided to link with a select range of outside bodies and relevant individuals. Consultation involved giving an overview of the scope and objectives of the project and inviting initial constructive advice and insights. To this end consultative support, advice and direction was sought from the following:

- The Management of the Limerick Travellers Development Group;
- Irish Traveller Movement Education Working Group;
- Resource Teacher for Travellers in Limerick City;
- Department of Education, Mary Immaculate College of Education.

## Setting up Working Structures and Principles

Each member of the working group brought her own particular skills, knowledge, understandings, attitudes and cultural perspectives to the process. Acknowledging and respecting the diverse capabilities that existed within the group was central to the establishment of the equality in partnership. A multiplicity of insight and wisdom existed within the group. Traveller members brought a richness of personal experience and understanding of what it means to be a Traveller. They offered the process direct and immediate insight into Traveller culture and experiences of marginalisation and exclusion within all aspects of Irish society, including education. Heightened awareness of the barriers blocking fair and easy access to the educational system for Traveller parents and children ensured that fieldwork study remained focused and relevant to Traveller needs. The non-Traveller programme leader brought knowledge of qualitative research skills and methodologies, an understanding of the mechanism of the education system and an aptitude for the structuring and directing of the research training programme. A shared vision and hope that equality, inter-culturalism and respect for diversity would ultimately inform the policy and actions in the education provision for Travellers, united the group.

With time, formal structures emerged. The working group met twice weekly. The meetings were recorded and chaired. The chairing of the meetings was rotated within the group. The meetings took place either in Mary Immaculate College of Education or in the Limerick Travellers Development Group premises. Working structures evolved. It was agreed that the working structures should meet the collective needs of the group. To this end the following working principles emerged:

- Each member of the group shall be respected at all times.
- Each member has the right to have her views heard and acknowledged.
- Confidentiality shall be preserved at all times.
- Decisions shall be reached through consensus.
- Positive relationships with the group shall be safeguarded.
- Language shall be accessible to all.
- All members of the group shall be responsible for creating a climate of acceptance and trust.
- Each member of the group takes responsibility for her own learning.
- Structures shall be flexible and open to the possibility of change and adaptation.
- The process shall be empowering for all members of the group.

## Raising the Issues

A considerable amount of time and energy was given to exploring the generative themes and issues surrounding education and Travellers. Engagement in this process was a vital aspect of the study. It served to draw the group into a critical reflection and analysis of the education situation from the Traveller perspective. It also helped to raise and identify a range of issues that became central to actual fieldwork training. Trust within the working group was consolidated during these sessions.

The diversity in perspective between Traveller and settled members of the working group was evident. Language between Traveller and settled was often 'translated' and explored as the discourse deepened. Different values emerged that reflected particular ways of understanding and construing Traveller education. This was evidenced in the interplay between the programme leader and the other members of the group. The challenge to hold the common ground between what is valued in the world of academia and in the world of community development was a constant challenge. It was the creative holding of this tension, together with the dynamic between Traveller and settled, that gave this project its unique tenor. Diversity arose between Traveller members too. This diversity was voiced in the context of Traveller issues as some members held and expressed stronger views than others. All members of the group challenged and encouraged each other to move beyond their own cultural and intellectual comfort zones.

Several generative themes arose during these discourses. The most significant and dominant issues for the Traveller researchers are summarised below:

- Discrimination against Travellers.
- Implementation of the Integration policy in the provision of Traveller education.
- Withdrawal of Traveller children for learning support (especially during Irish classes).
- Promotion of Traveller culture by the education system.
- Provision of relevant and ongoing education support for Traveller parents.

- Relationship and communication between Traveller and school personnel.
- Visibility of Traveller 'voice' within the education system.
- Inclusion of Traveller culture in school textbooks or syllabi.

These issues were recorded and acted as a reference point and context for the development of the fieldwork training study and for the interpretation of the data from the research investigation.

### Developing the Action Plan

The initial 'getting to know you' and brainstorming sessions laid a strong foundation for the construction and development and design of the action plan. The group set out to clarify and define the 'what', the 'when', the 'where' and the 'why' of the research. The action plan can be presented in three distinct phases. Here we outline the progression of the phases and identify the particular tasks and general time frame for each phase of the programme.

**Phase I:** *Development and Design* (September 2001-June 2002)
This phase sought:
- to create a climate of trust and acceptance within the group.
- to develop and construct a needs-based research training programme.
- to train four Traveller women in qualitative research methodologies, design and development.
- to offer an opportunity for the women to apply the skills of qualitative research through conducting one-to-one semi-structured interviews.

**Phase 2:** *Data Interpretation and Analysis* (July 2002-June 2003)
This phase sought:
- to identify and track dominant themes/issues that emerged from the interviews.
- to analyse the interview data using AnnoTape computer programme.
- to interpret and contextualise the research data.

- to evaluate on an ongoing basis the group process and partnership working relationship.

**Phase 3:** *Presentation Study Findings and Participant Learning* (July 2003-June 2004)
This phase sought:
- to collaboratively compile the study findings and participant learnings.
- to evaluate the research-training study process, relationship and outcome.
- to offer recommendations and insights to inform future research into Traveller education.
- to offer recommendations and insights into cross cultural partnership working models.
- to ensure ownership of the findings within the local Traveller community through the appropriate dissemination of the study findings.

## Specific Training Sessions

The entire programme could in many ways be viewed as a form of 'training'. Training was a pivotal aspect of the project and was offered to the group on an ongoing basis. Development of the training programme was always needs-driven. The working group discussed the issues as they arose. Strategies and techniques for interviewing children were examined. The optimum age at which to interview a child, the usefulness of asking a Traveller child to draw during the interview, the best place for the interview, the length and frequency of interview, the follow-up to the schools and the parents were all explored. Some questions however kept popping up: 'How do we keep the questions clear and focused?' 'How do we put the child at her or his ease?' 'How will we deal with the unexpected in the child's answers?' 'Will we know what to do if the child became bored or disruptive?' 'What happens if we don't keep the questions open-ended?' 'How can we avoid being biased?' 'How do we honour the Traveller child's right to privacy?' 'How do we keep the language relevant to the Traveller child?' The practice of Travellers interviewing within their own community was hotly debated: 'Will a Traveller child chat to an adult Traveller in a formal context?' 'Will we be able to hold the confidentiality and what happens when/if we hear information that we may not want to hear?' 'Will the parents give their permission?' 'What will happen when we meet the children's parents during or after the interviews?' 'How will the schools receive us?' Working as a team brought its own set of concerns. These concerns centred on the importance of developing a sense of collective responsibility, working co-operatively, planning an interview strategy in advance of the interviews, being observed and judged, giving and receiving feedback. Specific training sessions aimed at addressing elements of the research were scheduled. The following table offers an overview of the training provided.

| Training Sessions | Field-Work Training Tasks | Post Field-Work Training Tasks |
|---|---|---|
| 1. *Research Design & Development* | Development of the research plan<br>Outlining the research question<br>Selection of the research sample<br>Selection of interview topics | Research fieldwork<br><br>Review and evaluation |
| 2. *Planning the Semi-Structured Interview with Traveller Children* | Development of interview-skills<br>Development of observation sheet<br>Interviewing children<br>Exploring interview methods and techniques | Analysis of interview techniques |
| 3. *Ethics and Research* | Development of parental consent form<br>Developing of confidentiality code of practice | Review of ethics issues |
| 4. *Technical Training* | Use of recording equipment | Evaluation of use and effectiveness of recording equipment |
| 5. *School Protocol & Setting up Interviews* | Introduction of the research team to schools<br>Arranging interview time frame | Review of interview experience |
| 6. *IT Training* | AnnoTape computer program | Analysis of interviews using AnnoTape program |
| 7. *Analysis and Presentation of Data* | Indexing interviews<br>Collating data | Documentation and interpretation of findings |
| 8. *Evaluation* | Process review<br>Research achievements<br>Learnings and limitations | Formulation of recommendations and actions |

**The Study**

*The Research Topics*

While Traveller children's experience of school was the main emphasis of the training study the group felt that to confine the interviews to the topic of school alone might offer a very narrow picture of the Traveller child. Children do not live in isolation. They develop a sense of who they are through their interactions with others and with the world around them. In order to get a broader picture of the Traveller child it was decided to widen the scope and to talk to the children about themselves and their family prior to talking to them about their experience of school.

A series of three research topics were therefore identified: self, home and school. The working group thought that this broader sweep might lend itself to a more in-depth interview experience for the Traveller researchers as well as yielding connections across a broader range of issues. The key questions in each topic were focused yet open-ended, 'Tell me about yourself', 'Tell me about your family', 'Tell me about your school day'. It was agreed that three intervews would be conducted. The first interview would focus on the child chatting about her/himself. The second would focus on family and home and the final interview would deal with school. Follow on questions were outlined carefully and painstakingly. Agreement of the full working group was always achieved before finalising any aspect of the research design.

*The Research Sample*

The research sample was drawn from the total number of Traveller children attending second class in Limerick city primary schools in the school year 2001-2002. All primary schools in Limerick city were contacted to ascertain the number of second class Traveller children on the roles for the school year for that period. Fourteen Traveller children fell into this category. This sample offered a good gender balance, a variety of Traveller families and sites and a range of mixed and single sexed schools. The working group felt that second class children would be open and amenable to conversation and might proffer more positive experiences of school than senior class children whose negative experiences of school may have become consolidated. By the time the interviews were conducted, however, several Traveller families had moved on or the children were no longer attending the schools. The final sample was reduced to **nine children – six boys and three girls**. Two children from the sample were only interviewed once. The family of one of the girls moved away from Limerick shortly after the first interview. Tragically, one of the boys died suddenly during the course of the study.

The research sample was drawn from five local primary schools. Two of these schools are situated in designated areas of disadvantage. Three of the schools are mixed-sex schools, the other two are single-sex schools – one all girls and one all boys. The nine children in the sample came from eight different Traveller families and were living in five different local Traveller sites. The children lived in a mixture of accommodation – some lived in houses on site, some in chalets on site, some in trailers on site and one in a trailer on the side of the road.

*The Interview Structure*

Two interview teams were formed. The interviews were conducted in pairs. The research sample was divided between each team. Care was taken to ensure that no member of the team interviewed a child who was an immediate relative (that is, son or daughter or a child from the same site as the interviewer). One person from each team took responsibility for observing the interviewee and the interviewer during the actual session. The second member of the team took responsibility for conducting the interview. Roles alternated throughout the interview process ensuring that each person gained experience both in interviewing and in observation. In the interest of continuity the same interviewer followed a particular child through all three interviews. At no stage did a child find her or himself being interviewed by two different people.

The confidentiality code of practice, outlined and agreed during the confidentiality training session was implemented during the interviews. It was agreed that particular information received through the course of the research regarding individuals, families, sites, circumstances, teachers, or schools would be treated with absolute confidentiality.

The semi-structured interview format was chosen. The working group decided that an unstructured interview would be difficult for a first-time trainee interviewer, while a very tightly structured interview would be too restrictive and might limit spontaneous engagement with the child. Three interview sessions were planned. Where possible the interviews took place on consecutive weeks. Each interview on average lasted somewhere between thirty-five and forty-five minutes. The interviews were recorded, using mini-disc recording equipment and a Dictaphone machine as a back up.

Most of the interviews took place in school during the normal school day. Principals and teachers facilitated the withdrawal of the children from the classroom. In the case of one school where permission to interview the children was not granted the interviews were conducted at home. When the interviews took place on site the child was interviewed in a vacant trailer.

*Additional Interview Supports*

Two additional supports were available for use during the interviews with the children. These supports were optional. One consisted of a blank 'book' called *My Picture Book* which was created by the working group specifically for the interviews. A second interview support consisted of a series of posters/photos/pictures which focused on cultural diversity and ethnicity.

*My Picture Book* was comprised of a series of A3 blank pages. Each page had a particular  heading (for example, 'This is Me'; 'This is My Family'; 'This is where I Live', and so on). A book was made for each child. *My Picture Book* was presented to each child as a special book that could be filled in as he/she wished. It was agreed that *My Picture Book* would be introduced if the interviewer thought it would be helpful in encouraging the child to talk more freely and extensively. Using the book therefore was left to the discretion of the interviewer.

While the issue of difference and ethnicity was not the main focus of the study it was nonetheless an issue that the working group felt might arise with the children. The group felt that it might be helpful if the interviewers had at their disposal some techniques for exploring the theme. It was decided therefore to gather together a series of pictures that could be used if and when the need presented itself. In 2001 Pavee Point began the 'Éist' project[2]. Part of the early years programme the project aims at promoting equality and diversity through the use of an anti-bias approach in early years training and practice. This programme developed a series of sequence picture cards for use with children around a range of diversity issues. These colour pictures are visually attractive and depict school children from different cultural backgrounds including Traveller children. The working group decided that some of these picture cards might be useful in exploring ethnicity. Other black and white Traveller specific pictures from the Limerick Travellers Development Group archives were compiled. These pictures showed a Traveller site, a Traveller family and Traveller children at school. Use of any of the above material during the interview was left to the discretion of the interviewer.

*Initial Contact With Schools*
The principals of the schools falling within the research sample were contacted. The programme leader made the initial contact over the phone. The objectives of the research study were explained and the schools were asked if they would be willing to facilitate an interview team of two to conduct a series of three interviews with second class Traveller children during the school day. When asked who would be conducting the interviews the schools were informed that the interview team was comprised of Traveller researchers. A positive response from all schools was received with the exception of one; in this case the school did not

---

2. Murray, Colette and Annie O'Doherty, (2001) *'Éist': Respecting diversity in early childhood care, education and training*, Pavee Point Publications, Dublin.

facilitate the interviews to take place on its premises. The children attending this school were interviewed in their own homes.

After this initial contact an appointment was made with each school principal to introduce the research team. The programme leader and the research team met with the principals. During this meeting the team engaged with the principals and arranged the times for the first interview. This meeting offered an occasion for the team to become familiar with the school setting and the staff. It also provided the school with an opportunity to talk to the team about the initiative and to seek answers to any queries or misgivings they might have had.

## *Reception in the Schools*

Some of the members of the research team found entering the schools in the role of researcher a formidable task. Many of them felt that the schools had difficulty in accepting them in a role other than that of Traveller parent and some teachers even wanted to sit in on the interviews, appearing very keen to know what exactly the children would be asked. While the research teams experienced some negativity, reception in the schools was generally positive. Many teachers and principals were friendly, open and welcoming. A positive reception reassured the research team and they in turn, ensured that they conducted themselves professionally at all times.

## *Ethical Issues and Parental Permission*

The working group received specific training on the issue of research ethics and children. This training raised a range of significant issues for the group such as invading Traveller privacy, members of the Traveller community interviewing 'their own', the Traveller child trusting the 'insider', Traveller community being 'used' for research, Traveller parents' reaction to the research team in their day-to-day interactions and socialising. Significant debate was generated. This discourse helped clarify the focus and intent of the research. A research statement, explaining what the study entailed was developed. This statement was read to the parents when parental permission was sought. Both parents of each child interviewed were asked to sign a parental consent form agreeing to allow their child to be interviewed.

The interview teams went to each of the sites. They explained the nature of the study, asked for parental consent and assured the parents of total confidentiality. The team experienced no opposition. No Traveller parent refused to sign the consent form. On interviewing the children the research team read or talked through a prepared statement to the child. This statement informed the child about the nature of the interview and reassured each child that their parents had been informed about the interviews and that they had given permission for them to be taken from class. At any time the children had a right to withdraw or be withdrawn from the interview process.

*The Interview Experience*

The research team found the experience of interviewing Traveller children a fascinating one. Much of what the children said resonated with the interviewers. They were surprised at how well the children chatted to them. The interviewers did find that some of the children were quite private and guarded in what they said. However, it was felt that this response was in line with the value that Travellers place on privacy around personal issues. Being Travellers themselves resulted in positive levels of trust being established between themselves and the children – that is, once the children identified who the interviewers were and could 'get the measure' of them, as it were!

Some issues arose around the technical use of the mini-discs and the Dictaphone machines. The mini-discs were not found to be user friendly and the children were very curious about them. At times the presence of the equipment acted as a barrier to the smooth flow of the interview. The observation sheets, while very helpful when the tapes malfunctioned, were not used as well as they could have been and they required a skill in summary writing that had not been part of the training. More time spent on listening back to the interviews between the sessions would have greatly increased the quality of the interviews, but neither time nor personnel were available for this exercise. Listening to the interviews during the data analysis, however, provided an invaluable opportunity to review and evaluate interview skills.

Not being allowed to conduct the research in one of the schools presented a set back for the working group. It was felt by some members of the group that the failure on this school's part to facilitate the research may have been influenced by the fact that the research team was comprised of members of the Traveller community. Members of the group felt that had it been a settled person conducting the interviews that access may have been granted. The experience was a disappointing one for the research team and much discussion ensued. In the interest of the overall good of the study it was decided by the working group not to challenge the school's decision and to proceed with interviewing the children from this school in their homes. This outcome, with hindsight, was viewed by some of the members of the group as an inadequate response to the experience.

*Data Analysis: IT AnnoTape Computer Program Training*
The interview data was recorded and analysed using AnnoTape computer program. AnnoTape was originally developed for ethnographic research and is used in qualitative research tasks. AnnoTape was chosen as an appropriate tool because it allowed the working group to work directly with the audio data and to analyse the material while still in the audio form. The value of AnnoTape was threefold. Firstly, it meant that the texts did not have to be transcribed and the actual audio data could be accessed directly at all times. Secondly, it meant that the richness, tone and texture of the interviews were retained. This facilitated the evaluation of the interview skills. Lastly, through a process called 'indexing', the AnnoTape allowed for the compilation of a database, which cross references key themes across all the audio records.

When the interviews were completed they were downloaded onto AnnoTape. Then the process of creating the database began. The working group decided what main themes or indexes were relevant to the investigation, other themes emerged as the interviews were listened to. Each interview team took responsibility for the interviews they conducted and under the supervision of the programme leader the teams listened to the audio records and applied the skill of creating the indexes. During these sessions the teams also evaluated their own interview skills and discussed issues as they arose. Observations on the interview, the attitude of the child, the style of the interviewer, the flow of questions and the interview context were noted.

*Data Analysis Strategy*
After the interview data was collated the job of analysis and interpretation began. The working group reviewed the data, considered the material, discussed the issues and then offered possible interpretations and analysis. Part 3 presents the outcome of this process. Each research topic is introduced briefly. This is followed by a selection of direct interview segments from the children. These segments were chosen by the working group and are offered as a sample of what the children typically said. The group is aware that the selection of any segment of interview material in this way is open to judgement and research bias. However, the interview segments give the reader direct access to the voice of the Traveller child. It allows the reader to experience at first hand what the child said, to see how the child formulated her/his thinking and to draw his/her own conclusion. The group felt that this was an essential element in the presentation of the study findings.

Each interview segment is followed by a commentary. The commentary situates the material within the context of Traveller culture. All members of the group worked collectively in the compilation of this interpretative section. The views presented in this section are the views of the group and are not representative of the Traveller community in general.

**Limitations of the Study**
The focus of this project was to train four Traveller women in qualitative research methods and design and to support them in the application of these skills in the field of educational research. While this aspect of the project has been enormously successful

we are nonetheless aware of certain limitations to the investigation. We acknowledge the following:

- That the researchers were first-time researchers. The Traveller researchers were applying skills that were newly acquired, therefore they may be seen to be lacking in fieldwork experience. However, in conducting this educational research they are breaking new ground in the area of Travellers interviewing Traveller children.

- That while the key research questions were open-ended some questions may have been phrased in a more closed fashion resulting in some questions that could be leading or biased. It is difficult to exclude some element of bias in any piece of research. Becoming aware of and critiquing such practice was part of the ongoing pre- and post-interview training. On reviewing the tapes the Traveller researchers became proficient in recognising the limitations to this practice.

- That the research data review and commentary has been compiled by a small group of Traveller researchers. This group does not purport to represent the views of the Traveller community as a whole. Developing the skill of data interpretation and contextualisation was an integral aspect of the research training.

- That while the data that has emerged from the study is very rich generalisations to the overall Traveller children community cannot be made. However, in highlighting dominant themes and issues of concern around Traveller children and their experience of primary school this study is an excellent reference point for further research into primary school Traveller children.

- That the sample size is small and local. Unfortunately circumstances beyond the control of the researchers affected the ultimate size of the sample.

- That the sample contained a greater number of boys than girls. Given the time at which the interviews were conducted this was beyond our control. For comparative reasons it would have been useful had there been an equal balance of boys and girls. Future research with Traveller children should be timed to correlate with peak periods in Traveller children's school attendance.

- That the study confines itself to the views and experiences of Traveller children only. This was the focus and the remit of this particular study. However, a comparative investigation between the school experiences of Traveller and settled children would be very valuable.

- That in presenting the interview data individual interviewee codes have not been disclosed. Themes within and across interviews were indexed and are presented in the data findings. Interviewee codes, however, have not been divulged. As Traveller children form a minority group within the school system coupled with the fact that the research sample was confined to second class pupils and was drawn from a local area, it was felt that the identity of individual children could be established. Therefore, in the interest of safeguarding the confidentiality of the children's responses it was decided to keep the code private. It is recognised that in making this decision a certain richness may be lost in how the data is considered.

- That the commentary presented on the research data, while situating the findings within the context of Traveller culture, does not place the findings within the context of a general literature review. It is acknowledged that to have framed this study through offering a literature review would have been very useful. However, our decision not to include one must be seen against the background of the ethos of the project. Consultation, agreement and partnership were foundational elements to the entire process. At no point in the programme were decisions made or tasks performed by any one member of the group to the exclusion of any other member/s. This was one of the greatest strengths of the research process. Including a literature review would have entailed discovering a method that would have continued this participatory engagement of all members. While this would have been very exciting it would also have been extremely time consuming and demanding on resources. Unfortunately neither time nor financial resources for the intensive training that this would have required were available to us. It would have been feasible for one member of the group to have independently performed this task. However, there was a deep concern that if this task were performed by one member alone it may have weakened the strong sense of collective ownership of the work that resides within the whole group.

# Part 3
# What The Children Said

The working group gave much consideration to how the data might be best presented. It was important that the data be presented in a manner that honoured the research process, was easily accessible to the general reader and that facilitated maximum exposé of the young Traveller voice. That ownership of the study resided with the entire group and not with one or two individual members was also crucial. It was essential therefore that the working group fully agreed on the method and format of the data write up. This process took a lot of deliberation and while time-consuming and intense proved to be very rewarding and worthwhile. Safeguarding the process ensured full participation and involvement by all members of the group, it reinforced each individual's responsibility for data presentation, it offered a forum for informed debate and discourse around Traveller issues and it strengthened the value of collective accountability.

The outcome of our deliberations was that the working group would review the interview data together, select the relevant extracts, discuss the context of the interview contents and formulate an agreed explanation and commentary. The programme leader would organise the material, write up the content and present it back to the working group for final confirmation and approval. Any appropriate changes or adjustment to the text were made at this point.

This section outlines the findings of the study on each of the interview research topics: Chatting about Myself; Chatting about My Family and My Home; Chatting about School.

Each research topic is introduced and set in context. Selected extracts from the children's interviews are then outlined. The extracts are presented without alteration to the original text. These extracts are offered as a *sample* of what the Traveller children typically said in the interviews. Finally a commentary is offered on the interview data. The function of the commentary is to place the data within the broader context of Traveller culture.

## The Children Chat About Themselves

This section of the interviews set out to gain a general insight and understanding of how the Traveller child describes her/himself; what he/she does/likes best; what makes her/him happy/sad; who his/her friends are and what they aspire to be when they get older. Open-ended key questions were posed: Tell me about yourself; How would you describe yourself?; What do you like/hate about yourself?; Tell me about your friends; What makes you happy?; What makes you sad?; What would you like to be when you grow up?

This topic was explored in the first interview. The overall aim of the first interview session was to engage the child in a conversation about her or himself.

### Myself
[The interviewer invited each child to chat about her/himself. Given that it was the child's first experience in being interviewed it was hoped that the child might find the topic an easy and enjoyable one to explore. The key question posed was: 'Tell me about yourself'. A series of follow on questions were posed. These varied somewhat according to the interviewer and how the child

answered the initial question. In the main, however, follow-on chattings focused on likes/dislikes, experience of sadness/happiness and aspirations for the future. The interview extracts are samples of what the children typically said. (C=Child I=Interviewer)]

I: *Tell me about yourself.*
(pause)
C: I'm fine. (pause)
I: Tell me a small bit.
C: (Long pause) I don't really know!

I: *Tell me about yourself.*
C: I'm clever (at horses)! [This phrase is used regularly by Travellers when describing someone who is skilled with horses.]

I: *Tell me a bit about yourself.*
C: I'm good at school, I'm good at driving horses and I'm good at painting and colouring.

I: *What do you like about yourself?*
C: Good!
I: You think you are good? How good are you?
(Long pause) (laughs)
C: Better than ye! (long laugh)

I: *Tell me a bit about yourself... what do you like about yourself?*
C: I can write properly.
I: You can write properly? What kind of things do you write?
C: Stories.
I: What kind of stories?
C: The teacher writes on the board and I have to copy it.

[When there was a poor response to the initial key question, the interviewer sometimes re-phrased the question.]
I: *How would you describe yourself?*
C: I'm a good hurler.

*I: How would you describe yourself?*
C: What does that mean?
I: Tell me about yourself.
C: I have red hair, I've greyish blue eyes.

*I: How would you describe yourself?*
C: I'm fast!

**My Likes and Dislikes**
*I: What do you like doing?*
C: I like riding my pony.

*I: What do you like doing?*
C: I like going to the shopping centre with my mother. I like doing the pallets with my daddy and bringing them out to the man.

*I: What do you like doing?*
C: Driving horses.
I: Is that what you do best?
C: (child nods )I looks after them all right and I feeds them with hay and I gives them water and jocks them.

*I: What do you like doing?*
C: Playing football.

*I: What do you do best?*
C: Playstation (at home) and the games.

C: I think ponies are best.
I: You think ponies are best?
C: 'Cause I was reared with the ponies.
I: You were reared with the ponies?
C: Of course I had to be reared with the horses because (names a person) was reared with the horses since he was small and now I have loads of horses since I was small.

*I: What do you do best?*
C: I can walk round my foal, I give her hay and water and keeps her in the shed behind the chalet.

*I: What do you do best?*
C: Do best?
I: Yeah!
C: Playing!

*I: What do you not like doing?*
C: When I'm not playing and doing my homework.

*I: What do you hate doing?*
C: I hates going to the shops every day.

**My Friends**
[In the course of this first interview the children were also asked to chat about their friends. Attempts were made to identify if the friends the children had came from the Traveller or the settled community. Some of the children brought up the topic of girl-boy friendships. The extracts that follow are typical of what the children said.]

*I: Tell me about your friends.*
C: They are good to play with me. (Child names three – two Settled children and one Traveller child ).
I: What games do you play together?
C: Following. (Long pause) That's it, we are not allowed to play football but we play hurling.

*I: Tell me about your friends.*
C: Mind your own business... that's my business!

*I: Who is your best friend?*
C: (child names a settled child) He is the fastest runner, he is a whippet, he passes everybody out.
[This child sees his best friend 'even Saturday and Sundays'. He then goes on to mention a second settled child.]

I: Does he go home with you, do you go to his house?

C: (Long pause) Yeah. He lives in (names estate).

I: *Who is your friend?*

C: (Child lists three names – all settled children.)

I: Are they friends at home?

C: No. They don't like, some of those lives in the Island, sometimes I go to the Island with my father and I'm able to play with them.

I: *What do you like doing with your friends, what games do you play?*

C: Knocker gawlai [knocking on doors and running away].

I: *Would you play with them?* [The child has been talking about playing with settled and Traveller children together.]

C: Yeah.

I: What games would you play?

C: We don't be playing any games, sometimes we do be playing, hurling, football, fighting, racing.

I: *What do you talk about with your friends?*

C: We talks! We play bulldog! We be talking about the men wrestling on the TV.

I: *What do you talk about with your friends?*

C: Ponies.

I: Anything else? What do you talk to your friend (settled child mentioned earlier) about?

C: Horses. [This settled child has a two year old 'midget' pony.]

I: *What do you talk about with your friends?*

C: We talks about mom and dads.

I: *What do you talk about with your friends?*

C: We sit on the wall and chat.

C: *Names two friends – (settled and Traveller)*
I: And are you good friends?
C: Yeah.
I: Do you play together?
C: Yeah! Following in school, we plays ponies, we jock ponies at home.

I: *There's all girls in your family. Would you like to be with the boys?*
C: No.
I: Why?
C: 'Cause you'd get a bad name.
[This is picked up again with the child later on in the interview.]
I: Would you like a friend that was a boy?
C: No.
I: Why?
C: Do you know when you play with boys they just say 'I'm going over to your horse' and then they torment my horse.
I: Is that why you won't play with them?
C: When my horse is still, they just kick him, and they, they annoy my foal, that's the reason why I don't play with them. I don't even bring my school friends over.
I: Yeah, because they hurt the foal?
C: Yeah, because my foal is only around two months age.
I: But if you knew a boy who wouldn't hurt your pony, would you bring him over and be his friend?
C: Yeah! If they wouldn't hurt my pony.
I: And you wouldn't get a bad name for playing with him then, would you?
C: No, because my father only bates me if I bring over 'bauld' (bold) boys and I don't bring them over.
I: Have you any friends who are boys?
C: No. Not yet.
I: Not yet... but you will?
C: If I find a quiet boy who wouldn't mess my foal.

I: *Do you play with (names girl)?*
C: No, she's only a girl!
I: You don't play with no girls? Why?
C: No, that's the why, only play with boys!

[One male child mentions girlfriends.]
C: ...But he (older cousin by five years) is spotting a good few of them... like he always shows me the girls.
I: Would you play with the girls?
C: Well he attacks them if I don't. (The child doesn't elaborate on this.)
[Later on the same child is asked.]
I: Do you talk to your sisters?
C: Yeah.
I: Is that different then?(to talking to 'girls')
C: They're my sisters!

## What Makes Me Happy and Sad
I: *What makes you sad?*
C: When my gran died and my uncles went to England.
I: What was your grandmother's name?
C: Small nan.
I: Was that sad for you?
C: Yeah (with feeling)!
I: Why was that sad for you?
C: 'Cause I loved her.
I: Did you?
C: Yeah.
I: Do you miss her?
C: Yeah. I wish she was still alive.

I: *Were you ever sad?*
C: Yeah, when big nan and little nan died (grandmothers who lived on the site).
I: What was it like when you were sad?
C: Cross.

I: *Tell me did anything upsetting ever happen to you?*
C: Ya!
I: When?
C: When, when my pony got sold (said with feeling).
I: Who sold your pony?
C: My, my father.
I: Why did he sell her?
C: He just 'solt' her!

I: *What is the worst thing that ever happened to you, that hurt you or upset you?*
C: When my horse fell. [In a later interview this child admits that 'my horses dying' is the worst thing that happened.]

I: *What makes you happy?*
C: What makes me happy, ah, doing something funny, doing something funny, I starts smiling.

I: *What makes you happy?*
C: When I walk into the shed she (pony) stands for me.
I: Anything else makes you happy, really, really happy?
C: My birthday, 'cause I get a cake.

C: I likes feeding them (horses), looking after them and catching them.
I: What makes you feel good about that?
C: 'Cause when you're yoking them and driving them, some of them is fast and some of them is slow, when you yoke them and drive them it's fun, 'cause you can hit them with the whips.

**What I'd Like To Be When I Grow Up**
I: *If you had a dream... when you get older what would you like to be?*
C: A builder.
I: A builder? (no answer)

I: *What would you like to be when you grow up?*
C: A mother.

I: You want to be a mother do you?
C: And then if my gran is still alive I'm going to mind her.

I: *What do you want to be when you get a big girl?*
C: Be a big girl?
I: Yeah.
C: Want to go the Pres. (Presentation school) and be a pop star.

I: *What would you like to be when you grow up?*
C: I'd love to be a farmer.
I: Would you? What's good about being a farmer?
C: You have horses and you have sheep, no, I don't want no sheep or no cows, just loads of horses.
[In a later interview this child reiterates that he would like to be a farmer, but then explains…]
C: No, not a farmer, I'd just like to be normal with horses.
I: You just want to be normal, and what is 'normal with horses'?
C: Like, you are not a farmer or anything.

## Commentary

When asked 'Tell me about yourself' the children generally did not respond with ease or comfort. Many were reluctant to talk about themselves personally at all! Others appeared to experience difficulty in describing themselves. Some children asked for the question to be repeated while others avoided the question altogether by making fun of it or by changing the subject. Rephrasing the question while helping to clarify what was being requested did not appear to make any substantial difference to the quality of the reply.

Answers that were given were frequently annunciated in short, clipped phrases such as 'I'm fine'; 'I'm good', I'm fast', 'I'm clever' with little elaboration despite strong encouragement from the interviewers. Many of the children responded to the question by talking about an activity. These children tended to focus on abilities that they considered themselves adept at such as being good at a certain subject in school or being good with horses or at hurling or painting.

Personal attributes or personal characteristics were not spoken of in any depth.

It is possible that the children were nervous about the interview or were confused by some of the questions. Perhaps they did not really understand what was being asked of them. However, there is the possibility that they did understand all too clearly, but were disinclined to reveal particular details about themselves. It was a deliberate decision on the part of the working group to begin the interviews with this topic on self. We felt that beginning with this theme would give the children an opportunity to engage in a non-threatening conversation and would help to lead them gently and gradually into the whole interview experience.

However, the children's hesitancy to describe and chat about themselves caused us to review this notion. The fact that the Traveller community can be very particular about sharing personal information about themselves, their families and their work was raised as an explanation for the children's hesitancy to open up. The children may have perceived the questions to be too invasive and intrusive. On hindsight it may have been unwise to have begun the interviews with this topic given the Traveller community's respect for privacy.

Alternatively, the children's difficulty in describing themselves may have stemmed from a poor self-image or a lack of familiarity in formulating and verbalising an image of themselves. Only one child, for example, described physical features with enthusiasm: 'I have red hair and greyish blue eyes'. While some children did describe themselves as 'clever' or 'fast' most did not elaborate on the personal characteristic or attribute.

All of the children, however, engaged enthusiastically with the question about what they like or did not like doing. They talked freely and openly about the things that they do frequently. Driving horses, playing football, riding ponies, playing games, writing, hurling, driving horses, painting and colouring and shopping in town were all listed. Many indicated an activity at which they considered themselves to be skilled. Caring for horses was the most frequent and most favoured activity mentioned.

Several of the children, both boys and girls, talked passionately about their horses or ponies, describing how they drive, jockey, yoke, saddle and feed them. Activities involving horses in fact dominated the discussion for most of the boys and the girls, though one girl chose shopping as her favourite activity.

Horses are a distinct characteristic of many Traveller families in Limerick. In the past horse dealing (breeding, selling, trading) was one of the main sources of the Traveller family's income. Today, while the economic aspect of the horses has lessened somewhat and recreational use has increased, horses are still an integral part of Traveller culture. Horse management assumes a priority and a status for many Limerick Traveller men and boys. As one of the Traveller researchers stated 'for Traveller boys to do without horses is like doing without their hands'. Traveller boys learn the trade from their fathers, older brothers or male relations. Time with the horses is time spent in the company of the father and the men-folk. The male child seeks and attains attention from his father through working alongside him with horses. Many Traveller boys are socialised into assuming responsibility for the caring and tending of the animals from a very young age and parental expectations of them can be high. Some Traveller girls in this study show a keen interest in the horses too. This is not always typical of Traveller girls. The fact that these girls, at the time of the study, came from all female households may have influenced their interest in horses.

However, the girls did chat about tasks more typically associated with Traveller girls. One of the girls talks about 'shopping' and 'going to the shops'. This, in contrast to working with horses, is very much 'women's work'. Shopping is an essential everyday activity for many Traveller families. Traveller girls are trained into the shopping routine early on in their lives. Many Traveller women make a distinction between 'shopping' and 'going to the shops'. The child states rather enthusiastically that she loves going to the shopping centre with her mother, but that she hates going to the shops everyday. Going to the shopping centre or to town to shop is a pleasant event for the child. It is associated with buying clothes and getting special treats. 'Going to the shops' on the other hand is the routine shopping that Traveller women do on a daily basis. Many young Limerick Traveller girls are taught how to buy and budget for the family and are encouraged to develop a sense of responsibility for the care of the family. Just as time with horses is time spent with the father and male folk; time spent shopping is time spent with the mother and Traveller women. The young girls learn the skill of budgeting by watching and imitating female family members. 'Going to the shops' for this child in the study implies work and taking on a degree of duty towards the family.

On reviewing the interview data it became apparent that the activities that the Traveller children in this study participate in are more likely to be ones that are central to Traveller family and culture such as horse management, family and child-care tasks rather than the more pleasurable activities normally associated with young children.

A few children (all boys) did talk about fun activities such as playing football, hurling and computer games. However, it was felt by the working group that special circumstances in the homes of some of these children may have influenced a move away from the engagement in the more traditional orientated Traveller activities. The boys who named games such as hurling and football were among the youngest children in large, predominately male, families. In their particular cases the older males may have dealt with the horses leaving the younger boys 'freer' to play. The boys, therefore, may not necessarily be asked to take on specific responsibility for the care of horses. In the past, where horse trading was practised by a Traveller family, there would have been sufficient work for the majority of Traveller boys to take up a role in the family trade. As it is becoming increasingly difficult for many to sustain the traditional modes of Traveller economy Traveller lifestyle is being forced to change and adapt. Horse trading, for instance, in these boys' families is no longer the main source of income. These boys' lack of involvement in the daily care of horses may be an indicator of the changes that are taking place in Traveller economy and lifestyle.

It is interesting to note that these boys talked about their play and playing differently to the other children interviewed. The playing pattern of these children may have been influenced by the fact that the site that they live on connects with a large housing estate. Access to and interaction with settled children from this estate is relatively easy. In fact these children talked about regularly playing with settled children both in and out of school. It is reasonable to assume therefore that in engaging with settled children these Traveller boys are more likely to participate in the local play and games happening around them. This, in conjunction with the boy's freer availability, may account for their keen interest and participation in games such as hurling and football.

One other boy talked about playing computer games. This was the only time that a child named a specific indoor game or activity. The child in this instance admits during the interviews that he is frequently at the receiving end of a lot of 'extras' and attention from his parents. While the child's father deals in horses, this child appears to have greater freedom to participate in 'play' than some other Traveller children in the study.

Overall for the Traveller children their sense of self appears to be strongly connected to their ability to perform certain tasks. In the main these tasks undertaken involved some degree of responsibility and were central to Traveller life and culture. The children's inability to describe personal qualities generated much discussion. It was remarked by the Traveller researchers that in some Traveller homes children are more likely to be praised or singled out for *what* they do (or indeed don't do) rather than for *who* they are. It was felt that many Traveller children would not be used to having personal attributes named and affirmed. Given the complex context of the lives of many Traveller parents it may be difficult for them to find the time and space to affirm and nurture self-worth in their children.

In the course of this first interview, all the children were asked to talk about the times when they were happy or sad. Many of the children engaged with this subject. In the main their responses to the experience of sadness again reflect familiar sets of concerns central to the Traveller life – horses and family. Some children cited separation from family, illness and death of a grandparent as sad occasions. However, death, illness or selling of a horse were also strongly stated by many children as times of sadness and loneliness. Conversely, driving and jocking horses, knowing that a horse will come when called, being funny and celebrating birthdays were cited as experiences that made the children happy.

Respect for the family holds a dominant value within Traveller culture. Traveller children are taught about the importance of family from the cradle. Family in Traveller culture encompasses the extended family and is inclusive of grandparents. Grandparents play a significant role in Traveller life. Typically the Traveller grandparent lives within the Traveller community and is taken care of at home during old age. It would be the exception to the rule for a Traveller to place a parent in nursing home care. Grandparents are seen as a natural extension of the mother and father. In a large Traveller family the grandmother helps out with household and childcare tasks. In our discussion of this data Traveller researchers recounted how they tell their own children to 'go over to your nana', when they themselves need space and a break. Traveller women would rely on the wisdom, advice and experience of their parents. The centrality of grandparents to Traveller culture would be transferred to the children. Traveller parents would demand that their children show respect and love for their grandparents. In the words of one Traveller researcher 'the children would be murdered for giving back cheek to a grandparent'. It is not surprising then when some children in this study mention their grandparent's death as a time of sadness. It is interesting to note that the children who did not mention a grandparent's death as an occasion of sadness were children who did not have immediate access to their grandparents or whose grandparents were dead prior to their birth. For these children the experience of sadness revolved around the sale, illness or death of a pony or horse.

The limited range of examples from the children about what makes them sad/happy may indicate that for the Traveller children their lives revolve around basic, daily living where there may be little time or space for them to acknowledge or identify other sources of their happiness or sadness. On the other hand, it may also indicate that these particular children are not familiar with thinking or talking about such matters or that they would have benefited from greater interview time within which to explore such experiences.

In some of the interviews the conversation lead the children to talk about what they would like to be when they grew up. One of the boys talked about wanting to be a 'farmer of horses' while one of the girls wants to be 'a mother'. The desire to follow in, the parent's footsteps into traditional Traveller roles is still apparently strong. A 'farmer' to a Traveller child would be someone who has land or who has regular access to grazing for horses. This child is very adamant that he does not want to be a farmer in the traditional sense of farming. He just wants to have 'loads of horses'!

Aspiring to motherhood, on the other hand, remains common among many young Traveller girls. The traditional desire of a young girl to become well-skilled in caring for the family, get a good husband and have a family of her own is reflected in one female child's response. Looking after her grandmother has already been accepted by this child as her role. Many Traveller girls and daughters are encouraged to look after others. The welfare of siblings, parents and grandparents within the Traveller community frequently lies in the hands of daughters and daughters-in-law.

Finally, two children mention non-traditional careers – a builder and a pop star. As the child who mentioned wanting to be a builder would not elaborate it is difficult to see if this reflects a shift from traditional Traveller roles. The child who wishes to be a pop star talked enthusiastically about her favourite pop singers and even sang herself!

All the children talked about having friends. They talked about friends at home and friends at school. Friends at home for both the boys and girls were predominantly Traveller friends. Friends at school were a mixture of Traveller and settled. (This topic is explored again under 'friends in school' and can be found in Part 3, Section 3.3.)

When chatting about interaction with friends it would appear that for some of the interviewees there is a good level of integration with settled children. Several of the Traveller children make specific reference to settled children. At first glance this is viewed as a positive development in the inter-relationship between Traveller and settled. However, a closer scrutiny of the context within which the mixing of Traveller and settled is cited by the interviewees may help to gain a fuller understanding of the often complex dynamic between Traveller children and settled children.

Some children, mainly boys, talked of having settled and Traveller friends at home. In the case of these children particular circumstances prevail which may facilitate the integration between settled and Traveller friendships. For these children their site borders onto a large housing estate. Some family members have married into this estate. The estate is classed as a 'designated area of disadvantage'. People from this area would often encounter discrimination and marginalisation at both individual and systemic levels. Settled people and Travellers in this estate therefore share a common experience and are, in the words of the Traveller researchers, 'all in the one boat'. This, together with the inter-marriage between Traveller and settled community, may account for the degree of integration that appears to exist between settled and Traveller children interviewed from this area. The same degree of integration was less evident when a Traveller site was located near a middle- or upper-class housing estate.

One child who talks about having a mixture of Traveller and settled friends does so in the context of going to 'The Island' (an area in old Limerick) with his father. He states that when he goes there he plays with children from the area, some of whom are identified as settled and others as Traveller. The impression is formed that good cross-community integration exists. However, closer examination reveals that a number of families who live in 'The Island' are made up of mixed settled and Traveller marriages or are Traveller families living in houses. What appears then to be integration between the two communities may in fact be interaction between Traveller families themselves. So when this child chats about playing with the children in 'The Island' he may in fact be engaging with members of his own extended family. In contrast, the girls in the study tended to have settled friends in school and Traveller friends almost exclusively at home.

When reflecting on a statement from one child who talked about his friends being '*good* to play with me' a very interesting debate arose within the working group. The Traveller researchers viewed the term 'good' in the child's statement to hold strong negative connotations. From their experience of their own families it was considered that many Traveller children feel under compliment to settled children for playing with them; a complex interplay frequently exists between settled-Traveller friendships. Traveller children may make friends with settled children at school in order to 'keep in with them' or because it may make life easier for them. It was felt that a Traveller child would not say that another Traveller child was 'good' to play with her/him. It would be assumed that Traveller friendships were easily available to them. Further research needs to be undertaken to investigate the nature and quality of Traveller-settled friendships.

In some of the interviews conversation about friends developed into a discussion around girl-boy friendships within the Traveller community. The children's replies tended to reflect the more traditional practice regarding the appropriate interplay between Traveller girls and Traveller boys. In the case of the children who brought this topic up free interaction between Traveller boys and Traveller girls did not seem to be acceptable. In Traveller tradition children are taught from an early age only to interact with girls and boys from their own site or from their own close family circle. Play between the sexes is discouraged unless the children are related to one another. In the words of the Traveller researchers, many Traveller girls are told by their mothers to 'stay away from the boys' and to mind their 'character'. Mixing with non-family boys would incur disapproval from many Traveller parents. As one child states, a girl would get 'a bad name'. A daughter would be chastised by her father or her mother for playing with 'bauld boys'. A Traveller girl's future can depend on her 'reputation'. On the other hand, Traveller boys from the age of eight years onwards tend to separate out from the mother and move into the men's world of scrap or horses and begin to associate 'only with the boys'. It is in this male world that the Traveller boy typically learns what it means to be a Traveller man. It would appear from some of the boys' responses, that it is in this male world that the Traveller boy learns the skill of 'spotting' the girls! It is interesting to note that many of the children interviewed echo the more traditional views of Traveller culture despite the fact that changes in the area of sexuality and gender relations within the general community are beginning to impact on traditional Traveller values and lifestyle.

## The Children Chat about Family and Home

The second interview focused on the topic of family and home. It was hoped that any insights revealed in this interview would offer a wider understanding of the child and give a backdrop to the child's conversations around school experience.

The key questions posed to the children were: Tell me about your family; Tell me about your day at home; Tell me about where you live; What do you like about where you live?; What do you dislike about where you live?

### My Family
[Each child interviewed more than once was given the opportunity to chat about his/her family and the place where he/she lived. While engaging with the children on these topics the Traveller researchers were very aware of the sensitive nature with which these topics may be held by Traveller children. When the children were reluctant to chat directly about the family they were asked to chat about the sort of things they liked to do in and around home.]

I: *Tell me about your family?*
C: What do you want to know?

*I: Tell me about your family?*
[The child answers in relation to place in family and lists the members in the family.]

*I: Who do you live with at home?*
C: That's my business!

*I: What do you like best about your family?*
C: Going to the pictures.

*I: What do you like about your family?*
C: Ah... 'cause they're very nice!

**My Parents**
[In chatting about family some children mention their parents. Most of the extracts below come from the second interview. However, some extracts emerged in the final interview when the children talked about school and holding and keeping confidences. Many of the children talk about their parents in the context of helping or working with them, confiding in them, being grounded by them and getting parental help with homework. One interviewee talks about a child whose father no longer lives at home. The child is being reared solely by the mother.]

*I: Do you help your father at home?*
C: Yeah!
I: Doing what?
C: Shoeing horses!
I: How many horses would you shoe?
C: How many comes!

*I: If you had a secret who would you tell?*
C: I'd tell my father and my mother.
I: Would they listen to you?
C: Yeah!
I: Would they tell anyone?
C: I don't know!

I: *If you had a secret who would you tell?*
C: My mother.
I: Why would you tell your mother, tell me?
C: Because she would keep it.

I: *If you had a secret who would you tell?*
C: My mother, she wouldn't tell no one, my mother is very good to keep a secret... even if I say something about my father she'll keep the secret. Do you know what she always does? She always don't tell my father even when I robs his oats. I tell him I get my own, then I robs his!
I: And she (mother) won't tell him?
C: No!

[Child is talking about parental reaction to school fighting.]
C: Last summer I was fighting in the school and I got grounded (by parents) for twenty-four hours. I was fighting in the school with the young fellows.

I: *What about your homework, who helps you with your homework?*
C: My mother helps me with my homework.

**My Cousins**
[One child talks about his cousin who is an only child. This child is being reared by his mother.]
I: He has no dad back here? How do you think he feels with no dad?
C: He feels better!
I: He feels better with no dad?
C: Sometimes you know like, he feels lonesome!
[The child goes on to say that it is his job to 'smarten' up his cousin.]
I: How do you make him smart?
C: By bringing him off on ponies, cycling bikes, getting him hardy by hitting him.

**My Grandparents**
[Several children mentioned grandparents. Illness, death and anniversary Masses are the contexts in which grandparents were discussed. All chat about grandparents was positive with the exception of one child who talked negatively about a grandfather.]

[Child has been talking about his grandfather. He calls his grandfather by his first name.]
I: Do you like your grandfather?
C: Yeah!
I: Do you get on well?
C: Sometimes we do, sometimes we don't!
I: Do you do things together?
C: Yeah, we goes with the horses to (names a place in Limerick) out to (names another Traveller).

*I: Do you like your grandfather?*
C: He is a mongrel. I hate him!

[Chatting about an anniversary Mass for a grandfather.]
I: Did you go to that Mass?
C: When I made my communion, he, he died on the eighteenth, and I was taking off, you know my clothes and I went to the Mass.

[Child is talking about grandparent who is unwell.]
C: She (grandmother) is not very well.
I: She is not well at all?
C: She has gallstones and kidneys, she is in and out of hospital. I says prayers for her at home and I goes into the church in the chapel and I says a prayer for her.

**Where I Live**
[The children were asked to talk about where they lived. All the children interviewed more than once responded to this question.]

*I: Tell me about where you live. What kind of place is that?*
C: There is a fence around it and there is horses in the fence.

I: *Tell me about the site where you live.*
C: I think it is the dirtiest in all Ireland.
I: Why is it dirty?
C: Over (names a man) and all his engines and rats.

I: *Where do you live?*
C: Child names site.
I: What is it like?
C: I think it's boring.
I: Why?
C: 'Cause I hates it.
I: Why?
C: It's too dirty, the outside and I never brings my pony up.

I: *You're in a house?*
C: Yeah!
I: Do you like living in a house or would you like to be in a trailer?
C: Trailer.
I: Why?
C: Because you'd be able to move away in a trailer; you can't when you are in a house.

I: *Do you like where you live?*
C: Yeah!
I: You do?
C: No!
I: Where would you like to live?
C: A place, anywhere where you can have peace and quiet.
I: Peace and quiet, is it not quiet up there? (No answer. The child shuts down completely.)

I: *Where do you live?*
C: Down in (names the site).
I: Do you like where you live?
C: No I hate it!

I: What do you hate about it?
C: It's too dirty.

I: *Where do you live?*
C: We had to leave, we used to live in a village.

I: *Where do you live?*
C: (Names site) I live in a caravan.
I: Do you like living in a caravan?
C: No, not really, getting a house soon, in December.
I: Are you looking forward to that?
C: No, not really. I just want to sleep in a house because it is more better, because do you know the trailers? They gets all stuffy that's the why I don't like them really much.
I: Does any of your friends live in trailers?
C: Cousins.
I: Why do you think it is better to live in a house?
C: Because it's more better.

I: *Do you live in a house?*
C: No.
I: What do you live in?
C: A chalet.
I: Do you like living in a chalet?
C: Yeah!
I: Would you like to live in a house?
C: Yeah!
I: Would you? What kind of house would you like to live in?
C: A big house with loads of bedrooms, loads of bedrooms with all my work things in it.
I: What would be the difference (between a house and a chalet)?
C: You'd have your own room and stuff.

**What I Like Doing at Home**
I: *What do you like doing at home?*
C: Jocking my pony, me and (names a Traveller child).

*I: What do you like to do at home?*
C: At home?
*I: Yeah.*
C: I like driving horses, I like playing around.

[Child has been chatting about what she likes doing at home.]
C: I'm going to make a cake today, I'm allowed to bake, 'cause I know how to bake!
[Child goes on to tell how exactly she makes the cake!]

*I: What do you like doing at home?*
C: Playing games and doing things with my pony.

*I: When you go home (from school) what do you do?*
C: First I clean the yard and then I go inside.

*I: Would you have jobs at home?*
C: Cleaning the yard, checking my pony.
I: And who would help you clean the yard?
C: I do it with my father.

**Commentary**
Many children began the discussion of their family by recounting the number of children in it and naming their place within the family. One child began to name out her fourteen brothers and sisters! All children who mentioned family members were able to account for their position within the family – for one child that meant knowing that he was the second youngest of a family of twenty-three.

In line with talking personally about themselves, Traveller children can be very cautious about giving details of their family and home to non-family members. The Traveller researchers experienced this caution in most of the children they interviewed. Some children were tentative around family issues. Some were reluctant to talk about their family at all. These children tended to give general or indirect answers. Some children changed the subject altogether. 'That's my business' was the retort from one child. This child gave a similar answer when he was asked in the first interview to talk about his friends. As Travellers the researchers were aware of the value and significance of privacy within Traveller culture and were sensitive in pursuing the topic with some children.

In line with previous data the children appeared to be more at ease chatting about home activities and jobs than describing the more abstract concept of what family or home means to them. Several children chatted freely about the home activities they enjoy and about the jobs they have responsibility for. The boys in the study were more inclined to chat about this than the girls. The activities mentioned by both were – cleaning the yard, caring for the horses/ponies, jockying horses, baking cakes, collecting pallets, and playing.

The jobs the children were involved in around the home were not divided along strict gender lines as one might have expected. One boy said that he did housework for his mother, though he didn't elaborate on what he did, while some of the girls mentioned doing what might typically be called 'men's' work – collecting pallets and cleaning the yard.

In general the boys in the research are deeply involved with 'driving and jockying' horses with the men and the fathers. Driving, jocking horses and shoeing horses are generally a man's task. Responsibility for keeping the yard clean and tidy is normally taken on by male Travellers. Traveller boys would be brought up to take on this job. The girls who mention helping with pallets and having responsibility for cleaning the yard come from all female households. For this reason they may not be typical of Traveller girls in general. These girls however also mention baking (cited above), shopping and dressmaking (cited in previous extracts) as tasks they perform at home. From around the age of eight onwards many Traveller girls would be encouraged to take on 'inside work' such as minding children, cooking, cleaning the trailer/chalet and shopping. This is reflected in some of the tasks referred to by the girls in this study.

The children were not asked to chat directly about particular family members. However, over the course of the three interviews certain family members were named. Family members most frequently cited were father, mother and grandparents. A few children chatted about their cousins.

Interaction with fathers for both the boys and the girls in this study tended to revolve around activities with horses and pallets, though some children remarked on times they have gone swimming with their fathers. Mothers were talked about more frequently than fathers and were seen as people to be trusted and to whom secrets could be told. There was a sense that the children took the mother into their confidence because she would not tell the secret to anyone 'not even my father'. In the final interview one child discusses how it is his mother who approaches teachers around school issues. Several children named their mother as the person who helps them with their homework.

Mothers play a significant and defined role within most Traveller families. The mother is central to the effective functioning of the family. Traditionally she is responsible for the welfare of the entire family. Childcare would be viewed as essentially women's work. Many Traveller women, having the day-to-day responsibility for the children would typically form close and deep bonds with their children. It is not surprising therefore that for the most part the children in this research appear to reflect a close relationship and connection with the mother and a more distant job-focused relationship with the father. Mothers would be frequently cast in the role of mediator between the father and the children. Many Traveller children would be more likely to approach the mother in the first instance when faced with a problem. Only in exceptional circumstances would many Traveller mothers draw the father in to resolve an issue. The example that one child gives where he is strongly reprimanded for school fighting is such an illustration.

One child talks frequently about a young male cousin who is being reared by his mother. The experience of being reared solely by the mother in the absence of a father may make a Traveller boy appear 'different'. This was reflected in views of the interviewee. This child feels that his cousin is in need of being 'smartened up'. When asked how he might 'smarten' his cousin up the child responded 'by bringing him off on the ponies, cycling bikes, getting him hardy by hitting him'. Within the Traveller community a male child without a father can often be viewed, in the words of Traveller researchers, as 'soft' or a 'suck'. Such a child can also be a target for ridicule and bullying by other Traveller children. The child in the interview has apparently taken on the role of 'toughning' up his cousin. The relationship between this child and his cousin as evidenced throughout the interviews is very ambivalent.

Apart from parents, grandparents were the other main family member that was highlighted frequently by the children. Grandparents are central to the Traveller family structure and are honoured in both life and in death. The interviews reflect how the children in the study have been socialised into honouring and valuing the role of grandparents within their community.

Anniversary Masses, praying for the dead and for the sick, visiting holy places or meeting a holy person, would be a familiar aspect of life for most Traveller children. Children in many Traveller families would still be expected to participate in religious family events, many of which for the children in this study revolved around a grandparent.

The majority of the children expressed negative views about where they live. The provision of adequate and appropriate accommodation is an ongoing struggle for the local Traveller community in Limerick city/county. Many Travellers in Limerick seek accommodation that facilitates involvement in traditional Traveller economic activities such as horse-trading and scrap. Few local authorities provide suitable accommodation for scrap storage or horse management. As a result many Traveller homes, be they chalet, house or trailer, are situated close to the equipment and the materials required by Traveller men to sustain the Traveller economy.

The children's responses about their sites reflect the challenging accommodation issues that some Limerick Traveller children have to endure. It is not surprising that the children talk about the site being 'dirty' as the environs surrounding a trailer, chalet or house in the majority of accommodation available to

Limerick Travellers is wholly inadequate. The instance where the child mentions the site being dirty because of the 'engines' highlights how difficult it is to combine appropriate living quarters alongside a work-orientated environment. The presence of scrap and metal means that this child finds it difficult to keep clothes free from oil and grime. The child's concern over damaged clothes most likely reflects the Traveller mother's ongoing challenge to maintain appropriate levels of hygiene. Many Traveller women, however, while overseeing 'inside' cleanliness within the home, have little power over what happens 'outside' the trailer/house/chalet. It can be difficult for Traveller women to manage children in such restricted and unsuitable conditions.

Preference for a particular type of home varied among the children. Some children preferred to live in trailers as it was easier to move and travel. These children, however, were in the minority. Due to the lack of transient sites and the 'boulder policy' that blocks traditional Traveller sites from being accessed, fewer Travellers move around the country as they did in the past. The experience of travelling would therefore be unfamiliar to many of the Traveller children in the study. One child, while considering himself a Traveller, said that his family was 'settled' because 'we don't travel round'.

Some children talked about wishing they lived in a house. Living in a house would give them more room for 'my stuff' and would be 'more better' because a house would be less 'stuffy' and 'would be bigger and wider and nicer inside.' Traveller children living in trailers, chalets or indeed small houses share a relatively restricted living space with the rest of the family. Most children would not have the luxury of their own particular or private space or bedroom where they might, for example, keep personal belongings or toys. For some of the children interviewed, living in a house would be less confining and would give them a greater degree of individual space and privacy.

Many Traveller children are taught the importance of sharing from a very early age. They learn to adapt to the needs of others and to 'give and take'. Many would not necessarily feel that they had the right to appropriate a particular toy or item to himself or herself alone. The fact that the children in this study are looking to a house to offer them greater privacy and protection for their possessions may indicate a shift away from the traditional Traveller family value of shared ownership. With greater integration and mixing between Traveller and settled as evidenced in the interviews some Traveller children may be drawn to the family circumstances they see portrayed by their settled peers.

## The Children Chat About School

A central focus of this research was to gain insight into Traveller children's experience of primary school. We wanted to hear whether schooling was a positive or negative experience for the children being interviewed.

The children were invited to talk about school. Some children did not respond to the key questions. In these instances the interviewers found themselves coming at the topic from a different angle by asking questions such as: 'what is the best day/worst day you ever had in school?' While the outcome of this question is somewhat different to the original key questions it did allow the conversation on positive and negative school experiences to emerge and be explored.

The key questions were: What is your school day like?; Tell me about a good day in school; Tell me about a bad day in school; What do you like most about school?; What do you hate most about school?; Tell me what happens in the schoolyard; Tell me about your teacher/s.

**What I like About School**
I: *What do you like about school?*
C: Playing football.
I: Is there anything else you like about school?
C: No! I like playing soccer.
I: Why do you like playing soccer?
C: 'Cause I can get a goal.

I: *What do you like about school?*
C: I don't know, I think I'd sooner be out of school.

I: *What do you like about school?*
C: Me and (Traveller child named) and (settled child named) play horses and following and that.

I: *Do you like school?*
C: No! It's too long.
I: What's too long about it?
C: You have to stay in school for twenty-five hours!

I: *Do you like school?*
C: No!
I: Why?
C: 'Cause it's too long and it's too boring.
I: You find the day too long in school?
C: Yeah!
I: What do you find boring about it?
C: Like you're reading books and you're not allowed to, you're only allowed to go out playing at lunchtime, you're not allowed do nothing like fun!

I: *What is your school day like?*
C: Bad except for Fridays. I do art.
I: Do you like art?
C: Yeah!
I: Why do you like art?
C: 'Cause of the colours!
I: What colours do you like best?
C: Pink and yellow, yellow is the colour of the sun and pink is my favourite colour and blue is the colour of the water and sky.

I: *What was your day like at school?*
C: Grand. (child does not elaborate)

I: *What was your day like at school?*
C: Today is the best day. It is swimming day!

I: *What is the best day you ever had in school?*
C: Sports day, sports day this year.
I: You love sports do you?
C: Before we go on holidays.

**What I Dislike About School**
I: *What do you hate about school?*
C: Spelling tests!

I: *Do you like what you do below in the classroom?*
C: Not really!
I: Why?
C: 'Cause it's just a little bit boring.
I: What do you find boring about it tell me?
C: Your hand gets tired from writing all the time.
I: And what else?
C: When you have hard sums to do you get a pain in your head, and you can't do it and you start to cry.
I: And what happens then when you start to cry?
C: Start to cry? You tell the teacher and the teacher helps you.

I: *What do you like about school?*
C: I like painting, I like colouring and drawing horses!

I: *What's a bad day in school like?*
C: When I didn't do my spelling test right. Got one spelling wrong so then I had to stand out for two hours!
I: You got one spelling wrong and you had to stand for two hours?
C: And if you got three spellings wrong you have to stand for eight hours!
I: Why do you think that the teacher tells you to stand out?
C: 'Cause she says 'you don't do them right at home'!

I: *Tell me a time when you felt bad.*
C: When I'm 'bould' (bold) and I gets detention.
I: How long would you be away for?
C: You know like, at the start of lunch, when the other boys are going out I get detention.
I: Oh you would be kept out from class?
C: No just am… just ammm… write down a few lines.
I: Oh, you would have to write down lines! And if you knew you would get lines would you still be bold?
C: I don't know.
I: What kind of lines?
C: 'I must stop talking', 'I must stop hitting the young fellows'!

I: *What would make school a good place for you to go to? What makes it a nice place for you?*
C: A nice place?
I: If you woke up in the morning and said 'I'd like school to be like that' what would it be like?
C: (Long pause) Good.
I: In what way would you like it to be good?
C: I'd like to have more friends.

**What School Is For**
[In the course of some interviews a few children chatted about the benefits gained by going to school. They talked about how they thought school would help them to get on in life. While this theme was not picked up with all the children the answers nevertheless are very revealing and informing.]

I: *Why are you in school?*
C: For to learn!
I: You learn?
C: Yeah!
I: What?
C: Learn reading, writing and colouring and to draw.
I: How does school help you?
C: (Sighs) How I made the dress is cause I learnt how to make

them in school. I have hundreds of dresses, there is all different models.

[The child had been chatting about his love of horses and wanting to be 'normal with horses']
*I: Do you feel that school is helping you to be the 'normal person' that you want to be?*
C: No (very definite in his response)!
I: Why?
C: 'Cause (big pause) when you want something the teacher always gives out to you and says 'go on and sit down on your table' (imitated with passion).
I: Ok, so why?
C: 'Cause most of the time my teacher is mad.

[Chatting about wanting to go to college. College in this instance is local secondary school.]
*I: In what way is school going to help you (go to college)?*
C: They help me to know all my sums and things.
I: Will you need to know all them before you go to college?
C: Yeah!
I: What else would you need to know?
C: All about parents and babies and things like that.
I: What would you need to know about babies and parents?
C: To mind babies, in case they fall out and you might grab them before they get a big bump in their heads.

**My School Subjects**
[The children were asked to name the school subjects they liked the most. Some children talked freely about this topic while others were slow to choose a subject. In such instances the interviewer went through the main subjects in the curriculum with the child. The majority of children listed specific subjects that they liked or disliked. Some qualified their choice, others did not. Reasons for their choice were outlined by just a few children.]

C: I'm good at maths. I know a sum that fourth class wouldn't do... will I write it up?

I: Do... write down there beside the house. [picture that the child was drawing]

C: No you can write on the blackboard. Three divided by twenty and the answer is... no that is wrong. Three divided by sixty and the answer is twenty because you get, say if I was dividing by three I'd give you twenty, you and me, and so the answer is twenty!

I: Very good!

C: I love maths. I love maths!

I: *We have covered maths and computers...*

C: And reading.

I: Oh reading. Do you like reading?

C: (No answer)

I: English?

C: And Irish!

I: Do you read Irish as well?

C: It's boring!

I: It's boring reading Irish. Can you read it, yeah?

C: No!

I: Have you always done Irish?

C: Since I was in seniors, yeah.

I: Are you catching up?

C: (No answer)

I: Why don't you like it?

C: Because I do be looking at the words and I don't know all the words.

I: It's too hard is it?

C: And in English, I, I'm at the top.

I: That's brilliant and do you mind being at the bottom (in Irish)?

C: I do mind, I don't know all the words, yeah I gets them all said out for me, you know like the fellow beside me said you know like, he tells me all the things like.

[The child is chatting about maths.]
C: It's too hard!
I: Why is it too hard?
C: 'Cause no one likes to get about a full page of sums to do and then you have to do a load of *Busy at Maths* and stuff after that then. I'm no good at those sums.

[Chatting about computers.]
I: Do you like the computer?
C: I like it when we gets to play on the PC.
I: Are you good at that?
C: Yeah... then you can play sums and all that and all the letters and stuff and basketball.

I: *When you are in class, what is your favourite subject?* [Question was misinterpreted at first and was rephrased a few times.]
C: Reading!
I: Do you read often?
C: Some days I reads loads of books!
I: What do you read about?
C: There is a book in there called *Black Beauty*.

I: *What subject do you like in school?* [Interviewer prompts by listing a few subjects, the child picks up on religion]
C: Religion!
I: Why do you like religion?
C: 'Cause you do lots of writing and you draw a picture of Jesus.
I: What makes religion more special than maths or Irish?
C: Drawing pictures.

I: *Do you like maths?*
C: No!
I: Why not?
C: She gives us hard sums.
I: And does she (teacher) help you?
C: No!

*I: What about your English?*
C: Sometimes I gets stuck in something, but she just moves away to a different lesson.

*I: What are you best at in school?*
C: Soccer!
I: Besides soccer, in the classroom are you good at doing your schoolwork?
C: Religion!

*I: Do you like writing?*
C: No!
I: Do you like English?
C: Yeah.
I: Why do you like English?
C: 'Cause when you, when you just say it, when you just say it it's kind of nice.
I: Is it?
C: Yeah!
I: What about religion?
C: Yeah, that's good as well.
I: What do you like about that?
C: 'Cause I love saying prayers and singing songs.

*I: You said that you didn't like sums, why don't you like sums?*
C: 'Cause the teacher writes up sums and she gives us hard sums.

**My Homework**
[The majority of the children interviewed more than once talked about doing their homework after school.]

[The child has been talking about a poor performance in a spelling test. The teacher gave out to the child about homework that was not done properly.]
C: 'Cause she says 'you don't do them right at home'!
I: You don't do your homework?

C: I do, I do, do my homework right, but teacher says I don't do it right at home, the teacher says I don't do it.

I: *So you don't like doing your homework?*
C: No!
I: Does someone help you at home?
C: No, I always does it myself, but sometimes they do.
I: Do you find it hard?
C: No, I like doing my spellings and stuff and sums.

I: *When you go home from school do you do your homework?*
C: Ya!
I: Does anyone help you with your homework?
C: No. I don't need it!
I: And do you have to do your homework?
C: Yep!
I: Why?
C: Because we always do our homework in the daytime.
I: Who always does their homework?
C: Me and my sisters.
I: Where do you do your homework?
C: In our, what you call it room, a room with tables and chairs.
I: And where is this room?
C: Inside my house upstairs turn left and turn in there it is a white door and you go in there...
I: So you do your homework. Would you help your brother and sisters if they didn't know? Would you? Or are they able to do the homework themselves?
C: No! My brother is really stuck in his homework, and I'm not!

I: *What about your homework, who helps you with your homework?*
C: My mother and sometimes my uncle. He knows how to read and write.

**My Teachers**
[All of the children interviewed more that once talk about their relationship with their teachers. The consistent themes that run

through the children's positive experiences with their teachers are class participation and involvement in activity-oriented classes and being let go out into the yard to run and play. One child highlights the trust and confidentiality between herself and her teacher. The children's negative experiences with teachers centre on poor interaction between the child and the teacher. Many of the children talk about their teacher shouting at them, getting cross/mad with them, treating them unfairly, punishing them and sending them to the principal.]

I: *Do you like your own teacher?*
C: Yeah! She always does art with us.

I: *What are your teachers like here?*
C: I hates them. I only like one (names teacher).
I: Why do you hate the rest of them?
C: Because they keep getting me into trouble when I run, they won't let me run either. When we do art they say 'colour that green now' and all the girls would have to do the trees in different colours.
I: Are they (names other teachers) nice?
C: No they're mongrels.
(The interviewer reacts surprised!)
C: They are too, they won't even let you run out there in the yard case you run you bang your head.
I: So you don't like them?
C: I hate them.
I: You like (names teacher mentioned at the beginning)?
C: Yeah! she lets you run. She lets everyone run!
[Later on in the interview when chatting about secrets the child says the following about the teacher she gets on will with.]
C: I tell (names favourite teacher) everything. She can keep a secret, she won't tell anyone she won't even tell her husband.

[Chatting about the child's love for maths.]
I: Is your maths teacher nice?
C: No!
I: Is she a good teacher?

C: She just gives me easy things 'cause she thinks I'm small.

I: She thinks you're small so she gives you easy sums.

C: Yeah.

I: And did you tell her that you're not small?

C: I just does the easy sums.

I: And would you tell her that you can do the harder ones?

C: No 'cause, 'cause ammm, she'd just say, 'no you can't, get them done. NOW!'

I: And she gives you the easy stuff?

C: Yeah and I don't even tell her, I just says ammm, and then she says, 'Ok, back to your class now'.


I: *Tell me about your favourite teacher?*

C: Sometimes she is mad at me and when the other teacher goes away she don't be at me at all.

I: Sometimes she gets mad?

C: Yeah, but this morning she always lets me play with the clay and collect all the clay and collect the books, if I want to.

I: And why would your other teacher be mad at you?

C: Because she hates me.

I: That teacher I met a while ago?

C: (Child names teacher) but (names teacher) is a nice teacher.

I: How come you have two teachers?

C: 'Cause I goes down to her class.


I: *And how do you get on with the teachers?*

C: They, they gets cross with me sometimes.

I: Why?

C: 'Cause the young fellows hits me and I hit them too.

I: Why do you hit the young fellows?

C: 'Cause they hits me.

I: And what is it about, how do you start arguing?

C: (tape unclear) If he pushes me and I push him back and he hits me and I hits him back and he tells the teacher.

I: What is the teacher's response to you?

C: (tape unclear) 'If I catch you'. The young fellow he'll tell the other young fellows and it starts a fight.

I: Ok and does the teacher punish the other young fellows as well?
C: No!
I: And why do you think she punishes you?
C: 'Cause I'm a Traveller.
I: 'Cause you're a Traveller?
C: She doesn't like Travellers!
I: How do know that?
C: 'Cause she hunted another Traveller out of third class.
I: Did she?
C: Ya!
I: Why did she do that?
C: 'Cause he kept hitting young fellows.
I: And why did he keep hitting young fellows?
C: That's the why he did.
I: Do you think you're treated good or bad?
C: Bad.
I: Ok, do all the teachers treat you the same way?
C: Yeah!
I: Would you like something done about these teachers treating you bad?
C: A new teacher!
I: You would like a new teacher; what kind of new teacher would you like... you know if I said in the morning ok – I'm going to get you a new teacher what kind of teacher would you like?
C: A nice teacher.
I: What would you see as nice?
C: She won't put me to the back of the class.
I: And what else?
C: That's all.

[Another child has been chatting about a time when a 'young fellow' took his glove, wouldn't give it back and threw it to others. The child retaliated by hitting the 'young fellow'.]
I: And would you not have told the teacher?
C: No!
I: Why?
C: I hate telling her!

I: Why do you hate telling?

C: I don't know... 'cause she would only get me detention, about a hundred lines as well.

*I: Do you like your teachers?*

C: Am... amm yeah, I only like about two.

I: Why do you like only two?

C: 'Cause there only about three nice ones, and the rest of them is kind of bad, ask them for something and they say 'no, get it yourself'.

[Chatting about teachers and school.]

C: (Names teacher) gives out to me and she gives out to me and makes me stand, and now, I don't 'cause I don't do nothing.

I: Do you feel if you were a better boy the teacher would be nicer to you?

C: Yeah, just most of the time anyway.

I: Most of the time anyway, would you feel happier in class then?

C: Yeah.

I: What would make you happier about it?

C: 'Cause (names teacher) wouldn't give out to me.

*I: Do you like (names teacher)?*

C: Yeah! She used to leave us play every time, she just leaves you play for about six minutes and then we go back to doing stuff again.

*I: Do you ask the teacher to help you? (with sums)*

C: Yeah! Then she helps me and then I just get mixed up again.

[Chatting about the teacher in learning support.]

C: And she helps me do my sums. I does all my sums, done that today.

[This child has been chatting about the fact that learning the words of the songs (for Holy Communion) is difficult. The child would not tell the teacher of the difficulty.]

C: (Teacher) fills the blackboard with writing and sums, we have to do them all and then we had to take out our folders and learn our words for that, and we have to sing again.

I: What did you find the hardest, the singing or learning your words?

C: Learning the words.

I: Why?

C: 'Cause they were hard words.

I: They were hard words, did you have no one to help you?

C: The teacher writes them up on the blackboard and the teacher says that, and we wouldn't know.

I: You wouldn't know? So would you put up your hand and says teacher, 'I don't know them words'?

C: No, the teacher says them out and you would say them after the teacher.

I: *In what ways is the teacher helping you?*

C: 'Cause when I get stuck in something I asks the teacher and the teacher tells me it.

I: So you feel the teacher is helping you in school?

C: Yeah.

I: And if you had a problem would you go up to the teacher and say 'teacher I don't understand how to do this'?

C: Yeah!

[The child has been talking about pet animals at home.]

I: Does the teacher ever ask you if you have animals?

C: Yeah! but I tell them nothing, because I don't like them. I tell (names favourite teacher) everything; she can keep a secret, she won't tell anyone she won't tell even her husband.

[The child is chatting about finding things hard in class and telling the teacher about the pain in her head.]

I: Do you tell your teacher you have a pain in your head?

C: Yeah!

I: And what does she say?

C: Ammmm 'take a rest'.

## Additional Learning Support

[All the children interviewed were accessing some form of additional learning support. While the research did not seek to isolate the children's experience of learning support it came out spontaneously in the course of the interviews from time to time. When it did the interviewer explored the theme with the child. The extracts included are from two children attending different schools. From the interview extracts below it would appear that one of the children is going to learning support with other settled children from her class. It is unclear whether the second child who chats about this issue is being withdrawn from class alone or along with a Traveller cousin. What is very clear, however, is that this child is extremely comfortable in the room in which the learning support is conducted. The room is very Traveller friendly displaying many posters and items relating to Traveller life and culture. This child appeared to be very proud of the room and wandered round it with great confidence and ease. Two boys attending a different school also talk very positively about going to supplementary tuition. They are withdrawn along with other children in the class. Unfortunately due to technical difficulties in the recording of the interviews direct quotations from these children are not possible.]

I: *What do you do when you come in here (room where learning support is held)?*

C: Read! That book with the teddy bear, *The Little Red Riding School House.*

I: Who else comes in here?

C: (Child names two settled children)

I: Are they your friends?

C: Yeah!

[Child is speaking about the learning support room.]

C: I remember this room (room where the learning support is held) since I was four!

I: How do you feel about coming up here?

C: Fine!

I: Do the rest of your friends come up here?

C: No!

I: Why don't they come up here?

C: Because (pause) … (names teacher) didn't collect them she only picked me.

I: So do you feel special coming up?

C: On Fridays I play with all the horses (the room has pictures of horses on the walls).

**My Principal**

[The research did not set out to investigate the children's relationship with the principal. However, many of the children talked spontaneously about the school principal in the course of talking about school in general.]

C: I likes (names principal). (Principal) is nice to me.

C: Oh God don't talk to me anymore about (names principal). Don't get me started, 'you're home now for ten days' (names principal) goes like Casper the ghost. (At this point the child mimics the raised voice of the principal.)

[Child is chatting about the fact that when he fights with the 'young fellows' the teacher sends him to the principal.]

I: *What is the principal like to you?*

C: (Names principal) gets cross.

I: Why does (principal) get cross with you?

C: For fighting young fellows.

I: And do you explain your side of the story?

C: (Principal) won't listen to me

I: But do you ever tell (principal)?

C: Yeah.

I: And what would (principal) say?

C: (Principal) says that's not true.

I: OK, and why do you think (principal) does that?

C: I don't know!

C: Do you know (child names the principal of the school)?

I: Yeah I met (principal) the other day when we came in for the interview.

C: That's the principal.
I: Do you like (names principal)?
C: No! I like the school but I don't like the teachers.
[This child quoted earlier says that she likes the teacher who does art.]

*I: Do you like (names the principal)?*
C: Yeah. I likes (principal) now 'cause I don't fight anymore and (principal) gives me copies.
I: Is (the principal) nice?
C: (Principal) is nice to me, but sometimes if you do something bold (principal) would give out to you, (principal) would ring the shades or (principal) would ring your mother about you.
I: What would you be hitting them (young fellows) for?
C: 'Cause they start pushing us.
I: And would you get into trouble over that?
C: We would. (Names principal) says 'you're not allowed', (principal) brings us over to the office and (principal) would give you thirty or forty lines.
I: And would (principal) punish the other young fellows as well?
C: No.
I: Why would (principal) just punish you?
C: Yeah, well like when you're after hitting each other.
I: Why would (principal) just punish you?
C: I don't know! But now I don't, I stops, I don't fight anymore, I plays with my friends, and (principal) gives me a new journal.

**My Friends in School**
[All the children interviewed more than once talk about friends at school. Only one child states that he has no friends at school and that he prefers Traveller friends to settled friends. This child is very unhappy in school and appears to be bullied by his peers thus causing him to retaliate aggressively. Apart from this child all the other children, both girls and boys, talk about having a mixture of Traveller and settled friends at school. Some of the children openly named their friends. The children who cited a strong level of integration between Traveller and settled children

were more likely to have a positive experience of school. Those who had no or few settled friends in school were more likely to have a negative or poor experience of school.]

I: *Tell me about your friends in school.*
C: Today my friend told lies about me.
I: In school?
C: Yeah!
I: Did you tell the teacher? (child nods) What did the teacher do?
C: She put her standing by the wall.
I: If she was your friend why did she do that?
C: I don't know!
I: Did it make you feel bad?
C: Sad a bit.
I: How many more friends have you?
C: I have loads of more friends.
I: Is everyone in your class your friend?
C: Except those two girls [had talked about two girls in her class who had told lies about her, she was very upset about this experience].

I: *Have you friends in class (naming two children previously mentioned by the child)?*
C: Yeah!
I: How do you get on with the rest of them?
C: I don't!
I: Why don't you get on with them?
C: Because they hits me.
I: Why do they hit you, do you think?
C: Sometimes they runs past me and falls and they tells the teacher I hits them.
I: Have you many best friends in the yard?
C: No!
I: Have you no friend who will play with you in the yard?
C: No!
I: How is it that no one plays with you?
C: (Child doesn't answer)

[Chatting about friends]
C: (Child names two friends – one Traveller and one settled)
I: And who is (interviewer names one child as she know that the other child mentioned is a first cousin)?
C: At school (meaning he is a friend at school).
I: Does he live where you live?
C: No! (child names estate)
I: And are you very good friends?
C: Yeah!
I: Do you play together?
C: Yeah!
I: What games do you play?
C: 'Following' in school.

*I: Have you any friends?*
C: Yeah in school.
I: Tell me about your friends.
C: I have (child mentions five boys – four are settled, one is a Traveller).
I: What do you play with your friends?
C: We play 'bulldog' and then we catch one another we say 'you are a bulldog' all right, then we just be talking.

[All the children interviewed more than once talked about fighting with friends. Most of the fighting was school-related though some happened at home. Fighting in the case of the boys tended to be very physical. For the girls fighting tended to be expressed verbally rather than physically, though one girl talks about hitting a friend for hurting her foal. Some of the children mention getting punished or grounded at home for fighting in school.]

C: Last time I was fighting in school I got grounded for twenty-four hours, I was fighting in school with the young fellows.
I: What was that over?
C: I was playing with the young fellows and he had, he took my glove, kept on throwing it, 'throwed' it over to another young

fellow and I 'kilt' the two of them, and I got grounded for twenty-four hours and I had (names boy) in a head lock as well.
I: You must be strong are you?
C: Not that strong.


[Chatting about friends fighting.]
[Child checks if the interviewer knows the child she is fighting with.]
C: Do you know her? (Names a child who the interviewer does not know.) Well she frightened my foal and I hit her.
I: Was she crying?
C: She nearly killed the foal, 'cause she hit him on his back only the day after he was borned, and I nearly killed her.


*I: Do you ever fight with your friends?*
C: Yeah.
I: What over?
C: 'Cause when the last one is up in the yard and so we don't be up in the yard, sometimes they start pushing us.
I: And would you get into trouble over that?
C: We would. (Names principal) says 'you're not allowed', (principal) would brings us over to the office and (principal) would give you thirty or forty lines.


[Chatting about fighting with her cousin.]
C: She (cousin) said a bad word.
I: Why did she say a bad word?
C: In front of my face!
I: That's a terrible thing to do!
C: I wanted to tell the teacher, but she got into BIG TROUBLE.
I: And were you glad she got into trouble?
C: Yeah! Yeah!
I: Why?
C: Because she said a bad word in front of my face!
I: And you got her in trouble?
C: No! She was in trouble, I didn't get her in trouble.

## Commentary

None of the Traveller children interviewed in this study talked enthusiastically or eagerly about school. Nearly all of them point to a non-classroom activity as the main source of their enjoyment. The formal classroom routine does not seem to appeal to them. To these children schooling brings physical confinement and restriction. The rhythm of a school day demands that children remain seated for considerable periods. This would appear to cause some difficulty for the Traveller children interviewed in this study – especially the Traveller boys.

That the Traveller children find the school day long and boring and wish to be outside is not surprising when looked at in the context of their background and their enjoyment of outdoor activities (presented in Part 3, Section 3.1). Many Traveller girls and boys tend to spend a significant amount of their time outdoors. For the Traveller boys who are involved in scrap and horses many of their significant jobs and activities are performed outside. Little time is spent indoors for many Traveller boys, nor indeed for young Traveller girls up to the age of about seven or eight. From around the age of nine it is a tradition in some Limerick Traveller families to start training young Traveller girls to remain indoors. The girls are taught to provide support to the mother around the house and to carry out child-minding tasks. However, even when it comes to childcare Traveller girls could still find themselves supervising their younger siblings outside as well as inside the trailer/chalet/house.

Freedom of movement and accessibility to outdoor space therefore appears to be extremely important to the Traveller children interviewed in this study. This is reflected in their responses. They all expressed a strong desire for activity of some kind. This need to be active cannot be separated from their cultural background and what, as stated by one of the Traveller researchers, 'is in their blood'. When mentioning the best day in school the children single out sports day, swimming day and the last day of school before holidays! Focusing on active interests is consistent with what these children discussed when talking about themselves in the first interview.

Engaging with the children around what they liked/disliked about school inevitably brought up the topic of school subjects. English reading and writing, PE, religion, maths, computers and swimming were selected as subjects that were most liked. The three subjects most disliked were maths, writing (English) and Irish. While some children enjoyed maths and English writing, no child mentioned Irish as a favourite subject.

Withdrawal of Traveller children from class for supplementary support was an issue that emerged from the interviews. It is the practice in many schools to withdraw Traveller children from the main class and to offer them additional educational guidance through learning support classes. All the Traveller children in this study were withdrawn from class for learning support. Most of the children did not seem to be aware of the significance of this procedure. Some of the children were withdrawn with settled children while others were withdrawn on their own or with other Travellers. Two boys attending the same school talked very positively about their experience of these classes. Indeed school in general for these two boys was a positive experience. (Unfortunately the direct responses from these children were not available due to technical difficulties in recording the interviews.)

However, withdrawal of only Traveller children from class is a contentious issue for many Traveller parents who perceive that their children are being withdrawn without a formal educational assessment or without clear parental consultation. Many feel that it is a given that if you are a Traveller you will be automatically withdrawn. Withdrawal of Traveller children may reinforce the Traveller child's poor perception of her or his ability to perform and may further isolate them from their school peers.

It is apparent from the extracts above that many of the children are struggling academically. Many of them display a due lack of confidence in themselves. More of them have become all too aware that their performance does not always match that of the class standard or of the teacher's expectations. Other children are aware of the importance of home support. Adequate support at home, however, was not available to all the children in this study. Inability to support a son or daughter's educational progress is inherently linked with poverty, inadequate accommodation provision and insufficient availability of regular strategies to help redress the low literacy among many Traveller parents. A lack of knowledge around the new primary school curriculum compounds the difficulties. All act as barriers to Traveller parents' effective involvement in the education of their children.

Homework is one means through which school can connect with parents. Some of the children in the study admitted to doing homework in the evenings after school. Some of the children received help while others were adamant that they did not need help from anyone at home. If help was given it was most likely to be given by the mother. One child mentions an uncle who helps her because she said he 'can read and write'. Another child talks about making an effort with the homework. However, from the child's perspective that effort was not recognised by the class teacher. The child talked about feeling reprimanded and criticised for doing the work 'incorrectly'.

Insight into how the Traveller children in this study view the significance of school and education can be gained from what they perceive school can or cannot do for them. The responses given on this issue are divided. The girls talk about school teaching them how to read and write and helping them to acquire dressmaking and child-care skills. One of these girls comes from a family where education and the acquisition of literacy and numeracy skills is highly valued and encouraged. On the other hand, one boy is adamant that school cannot help him in his pursuit to be 'normal with horses'; horses are this child's passion. It would appear that for him school has little relevance in helping him to achieve his ambition to work with horses. For this child school does not appear to meet with his long term needs.

The nature of the relationship between the Traveller children and their teachers is discussed during the interviews. A range of responses emerged on this topic. Some responses are positive, some negative. The children talked about 'the teacher/s', 'my teacher' 'the other teacher', 'my own teacher'. As all children in the study were accessing learning support it is reasonable to assume that they have had exposure to more than one teacher in school. This study did not seek to differentiate between the child's relationship with the class teacher and the teachers offering the learning support. However, the interview data points to a qualitative difference between the children's relationship with the class teacher and their relationship with the learning support teacher/s. The more positive comments on teachers seemed to be directed more towards the learning support teachers though this is inconclusive. The full extent of Traveller children accessing learning support in Limerick primary schools requires investigation. Such research, if undertaken, could also examine the nature of the pupil-teacher relationship in this specialised educational context.

Many of the children's responses, however, reflect a negative pupil-teacher relationship. This is true particularly of the boys in the study. Relationship with teachers is characterised by harsh communication, reprimands and punishment. When talking negatively about the teachers the children tend to use rather uncompromising language – 'I hates them', 'they hates me', 'they're mongrels'. This could be consistent with some Traveller children's tendency to use strong, direct language. Many of the children imitated the way the teachers talked to them. Any child who did this did so by using angry tones and raising their voices to a high pitch.

The teachers that were liked by the children in the research were teachers who gave frequent breaks, let them play and run in the yard, let them do art, treated everyone the same, kept secrets and who invited them to take responsibility for classroom tasks such as collecting books/clay in the classroom.

The question, 'would you ask your teacher for help if you needed it?' raised interesting responses. Some children felt free to inform the teacher about difficulties that they may be having. Some sought help and received it. One child talks about getting help with reading and writing. Another child says that she does get help from the teacher, but wouldn't ask for it. A few said that they would not ask a teacher for help. One child deliberately withholds information from the teacher. It would have been interesting to have ascertained if the teachers that the children trusted and found helpful were the child's class teacher or the learning support teacher/s. Some of the responses appear to indicate that the children experience difficulties in main classroom participation, for example 'the teacher writes them (words) up on the blackboard and the teacher says that, and we wouldn't know.' While other responses appear to indicate a learning support environment where individual time and attention is available to the child, for example 'and she helps me do my sums, does all my sums, done that today'.

Negative experiences of teachers in this study seem to outweigh the positive experiences. This may be due to the fact that the research sample consisted of more boys than girls. Boys in the study were more inclined to express dissatisfaction with school and teachers than the girls. However, for all of the children who talked negatively about their teachers, poor communication between the child and the teacher was a dominant factor. There is a sense in which some of the children do not feel listened to or feel that if they make a request it won't be granted, for instance, 'She'd say "no you can't, get them done now!"' The impression is given across all the interviews that the education system fails to acknowledge or highlight the children's positive attributes. If attributes are being affirmed they are not being taken on board by the children. At no point did any child mention being praised or affirmed. In fact the children seem to have begun to internalise and accept much of the negative criticisms of themselves and were holding themselves accountable, for example '(teacher) gives out to me and makes me stand, and now I don't 'cause I don't do nothing'.

While the research investigated the children's relationship with the teachers, the children's relationship with the school principal was not singled out for specific scrutiny. However, many of the children, especially the boys talked spontaneously about their experience of the school principal. Positive experiences centered on the principal treating the child in the 'same way as other children', being 'nice' to the child, and rewarding the child for improved behaviour. Some boys attending the same school talked in particular about their principal 'as friendly' and 'someone who treated them fairly'. (Unfortunately direct quotation from this interview was not possible because of technical difficulties). Negative remarks about the principal focused on the way the principal was seen to deal with behaviour such as coming late to school, bullying and fighting in the playground. A number of children mimicked the voice of the principal. They did so in a loud abrupt voice combined with a sharp, angry tone.

While the girls made passing references to their principal, most of the children who made remarks about a principal are boys. The topic of school principals for the boys emerged typically in relation to school fighting. The boys seemed to be very honest and forthright in their descriptions of fighting in school and in acknowledging the part they played in the scuffles with the 'young fellows'. They depict a situation where they physically fight with their peers in the school yard. They do so in an open, non-bragging manner. If they are up-front in their disclosure of their own aggressive behaviour one can reasonably assume that the experiences they relate about how their behaviour is dealt with by the school are honestly recounted. Who initiates the fighting is not always clear. The hitting and fighting may be a reaction by the Traveller boys to being bullied in the playground or the boys may instigate the fighting themselves. While these particular Traveller boys' aggressive behaviour cannot be denied the interviews reveal evidence of bullying taking place in the playground. One child talks about being pushed by other boys as he goes out into the school yard. Another boy talked about having his hat taken and thrown about by other children. In both instances the children retaliated by fighting back.

How the children, especially the boys, in this study perceived the principal to deal with them seems to colour the quality of the relationship. Those who talk positively about the principal are more likely to experience the principal as fair and friendly. The children who talk negatively about the principal are more likely to talk about experiencing discrimination, unfair treatment, and punishment. In listening to these children the impression is given that they feel particularly victimised and discriminated against when it comes to the school investigating and dealing with inappropriate behaviour between settled and Traveller children. The boys felt that the school did not deal fairly with everyone across the board when playground fighting was being checked. One child talks about the principal threatening to 'call the séids' (Gardaí). This sense of being discriminated against and being singled out for punishment over and above the settled child comes up time and again with a cluster of boys. One of the boys appears to have accepted that it is his responsibility to change in order to be accepted within the school system. In general for the boys in this study the quality of their relationship with the principal is an indicator of the child's attitude towards the school. Positive experiences of the principal appear to correlate with positive experiences and attitude towards school. The converse also appears to hold true. Negative experiences of the principal tend to correlate with negative experiences and attitude to school/schooling.

Establishing friendships is an essential element in any child's experience of school. When it comes to looking at school interaction most of the children interviewed formed friendships. Many seem to have a mixture of friends from both the settled and Traveller communities. The experiences with the settled friends appear to be positive (with the exception of the child who has few school friends and who feels isolated and mistreated). Where a child mentions a school friend who is a Traveller, the Traveller friend was usually related to the child.

It is interesting to note that the most positive integration between settled and Traveller occurs in a school where the Traveller site is situated alongside a main local authority housing estate. The children from this school, for whom schooling was in the main a positive experience, played with settled children in school and on the street after school. One of them talked about visiting the homes of settled children. These boys also named some settled children who come down to the site to play with them.

## Sub-Topics

A series of sub-topics emerged in the course of the interviews. While the topics were not the main focus of the study they nevertheless offer a further insight into the world and mind of the Traveller children who participated in the research. Each sub-topic is presented separately and followed by selected interview extracts.

**Travellers as Different**
[Whenever the opportunity presented itself the interviewer explored the topic of ethnic difference and Traveller identity with the children. Some children were asked if they thought that Travellers were different from other people and if so in what ways they were different. The majority of the children who explored this issue perceive Travellers to be different.

In order to stimulate a discussion around ethnic diversity a series of pictures (mentioned in Part 2, The Study: Additional Interview Supports) had been collated to use with the children during the interviews. These picture cards, for the most part, depicted a range of young, school-going children from diverse cultural backgrounds inclusive of Traveller children. Other Traveller-specific pictures were used. The Traveller-specific pictures were in black and white and showed a Traveller site, a Traveller family and some Traveller children in class at school. It was agreed by the working group that the pictures would be used at the discretion of each interviewer. Each interviewer would assess when or if it was appropriate to introduce the visuals. However it was also agreed that when a picture was presented for the first time, the child would be asked to simply describe what he/she saw in the picture. Chatting about ethnicity and diversity issues progressed from this starting point. While there may have been limitations to how the pictures were used the visual aids were successful in stimulating discussion on ethnic diversity. The variety of discussion that emerged from the children who engaged with this issue is mirrored in the quotations selected below.]

I: *What do you see in the picture?* (Picture of three children painting together – two white girls and one black boy.)
C: A black child.
I: Is he different?
C: Than all the other ones? Yeah!
I: How is he different?
C: He is different from all the other ones (said very quietly).
I: How is he different?
C: He is different than all them ones. One is black the other is white.
I: If he (the black child) was in your classroom now what would be different about him?
C: Nobody would play with him!
I: Why?
C: (Long pause) Well there is a few boys that would play with him.
I: Why would some of the kids not play with him?
C: If he was fast enough, if he could give us a chance he can play, but if he can't... [outside interruption happened at this point and the conversation was ended.]

I: *Do they look like Travellers?*
C: Well she does, she is wearing earrings.

I: *What is the difference between a Traveller girl and a country girl?*
C: Nothing.

I: *Are you different from the other young fellows that go to school?*
C: Yeah!
I: How?
C: They are country people.
I: And what's country people, tell me?
C: They lives in houses.
I: And what makes you a Traveller?
C: 'Cause I live in a chalet.

*I: Do you know these little children you go to school with, are they like ye, are they like yourself?*
C: Naw!
*I: What's different about them?*
C: Like some of them don't fight, I don't either, but some of them don't fight and they plays with you like and they have better colouring and painting and you look at theirs and their colouring is nicer.

[This extract follows on from a conversation about the interviewee's cousin. The child had been talking about her cousin relating how she doesn't come to school often and how she lives in a caravan on the roadside.]
*I: Do you think that (living in a caravan on the side of the road) makes her different to the rest of the children?*
C: Yeah! Maybe. I don't know!
*I: Why is she different, because she lives in a caravan?*
C: People don't, my friends don't really like, am, don't like friends living in caravans.
*I: So is she different from the rest of the friends?*
C: Yeah!
*I: What do her friends say about her?*
[The child goes on to say that her friends make very derogatory remarks about this. She tells exactly what the friends say but asked that the remarks be a 'secret between you (interviewer) and me'. For this reason the direct statements have not been included.]

[In the course of a conversation about school one child talks about 'buffers'. Buffer is a Traveller word for non-Traveller.]
*I: Why do you call the rest of the children buffers?*
C: Call them buffers.
*I: Yeah? Aren't they the same as you?*
C: No, but they're not Travellers.
*I: What is the difference between ye?*
C: They're buffers!
*I: I sees you lined up with the rest of the children just now I wouldn't know any difference. So tell me how do you feel different?*

C: I wouldn't like to be a buffer, they think they're cleaner. (Child suddenly ends the subject.)

I: *Tell me one good thing about Travellers.*
C: They have horses, some buffers has horses.
I: Yeah? And what else?
C: What do I like about Travellers?
I: Yeah. Well yeah… what's one good thing about Travellers?
C: Good, yeah they are nicer.

I: *Are you a settled or a Traveller child?*
C: Settled.
I: Are you? How do you know?
C: 'Cause I don't travel!

**Where I Sit in the Classroom**
[Some members of the working group saw the seating position of a Traveller child in the classroom as an indicator of fairness to or discrimination against the child. This issue was hotly debated within the working group. Full agreement was not reached on the centrality of the topic and, therefore, it did not become part of the main study. The issue arose, however, in three interviews. The responses are presented below.

The first interview segment comes from a child who was interviewed in the special room in the school designated for learning support. The child was familiar with the room and was relaxed and at home in this environment. The exact seating arrangement in the room is pointed out to the interviewer. This child however does not mention the seating arrangement in the formal classroom. The two other extracts are from children attending the school that did not facilitate the research team in conducting the interviews within the school. These children are talking about the seating arrangement in the main classroom.]

[The interviewer is chatting to the child about the room in which learning support is held. The interviews were conducted in this room. The child points to the desk where she sits in the room.]

C: See where the door is, see the second desk, I sit there with my friend.

I: *Where do you sit in the classroom?*
C: Over at the side.
I: And where is over at the side?
C: Row one, row two, row three, I sits on row three, three is the last row.
I: Would you like to sit at the front of the classroom?
C: No, I like to sit at the back of the classroom, near the computer.

I: *Where do you sit in the classroom?*
C: At the back of it.
I: At the back of it, why do you sit at the back of the classroom?
C: 'Cause.
I: Do you like being at the back of the classroom?
C: No.
I: Why not?
C: 'Cause she just puts you there for hitting the young fellows.
I: Would you feel you would learn more at the front of the class rather than at the back of the classroom?
C: Yeah!
I: Why would you, how would you know?
C: 'Cause I talks to people!

**Curiosity**
[Many of the Traveller children were very actively curious during the interviews. The focus of their curiosity ranged from enquiring about the equipment, to people, to the interviews themselves. The extracts give samples of what the children typically inquired about.]

C: Do you know my mother?
I: Yeah. I know her.

C: Do you know any of the (child names a particular Traveller family)?
I: I know (names a person) that's it.

C: Do you know my mother?
I: Mmm. Yeah.
C: Right so! Do you know my father?
I: Yep!

C: What is your husband's name?
I: (Interviewer tells the child her husband's name)
C: I saw him in McDonald's and I saw you and I saw your daughter!

C: Where do you live (asked of the interviewer)?
I: (Interviewer answers the child's question)
(Child then checks if the interviewer knows some people that she knows also.)

C: Do you know? (child names about five people. The people named are not from the child's site, but would visit her site often.)

C: Does (names teacher) really live up near you?

C: How many are you taking (children for interviews)?

C: Are you bringing all of us? Can I stay for break-time?

C: Can I stay longer?

C: Is this the last time you see me?
(This child checks if other children are being asked the same questions.)

C: Are you good at keeping a secret?

C: What's that for? (child is referring to the mini-disc)

C: Can I sing into the machine?

**Secrets**
[All the children interviewed more than once were asked in whom they would confide if they had a secret. Most children said that they would confide in their mother or their mother and father. One child said that he would not confide in anyone. One girl said that she does not like telling people about herself and what she does. Finally, other children mentioned a cousin, a friend and a teacher as their confidant. The key question was: 'If you had a secret who would you tell?']

C: Tell (names teacher) she won't tell anyone, she won't tell her husband.

C: My mother is very good to keep a secret, even if I say something about my father she'll keep the secret.

C: No one!

C: My mother.
I: Why would you tell your mother?
C: Because she would keep it.
I: Is she good to keep a secret?
C: Yeah, she wouldn't tell no one!

C: I'd tell my father and my mother.
I: Would they listen to you?
C: Yeah.
I: Would they tell anyone?
C: I don't know!

C: My friends.
I: Did you ever tell her a secret?
C: No, not really.

C: I don't like telling the other people what I do and secrets like that.

C: My cousin.

## Religion

[Religion featured in many of the children's interviews. The children chatted about how religion and prayers were important to them. One child talked about heaven and his deceased grandmother. Generally talk about religion centred around experiences of sickness, death, holy places and Holy Communion.]

[One child (boy) is talking about his grandmother who had died. He said that she is in heaven.]
I: Where is heaven?
C: Up there.
I: Where is up there?
C: Up there in the moon.
I: She (grandmother) is up there in the moon is she?
C: Yeah!

[One child (girl) is talking about her sick grandmother.]
C: I need to say a prayer for her in school and prayer at home and in the chapel inside the church I always goes there.
I: Say a prayer?
C: Do you know the holy place in Doon? I goes there.
I: And you pray for your nana?
C: Yeah! And did you go into the silent place?
I: No.
C: Did you go down to the holy pond?
I: Yeah, the well is it?
C: No, not the well, you walk into the garden.
I: No I don't know about that, what is it?
C: There is a little fish in it.
I: Do you like going in there?
C: Yeah and you are allowed bring in small babies as well, my friend, I have a friend out there; she brought me to see the fishes, she brought me into the pond.
I: The girl's name is Fiona (this is the 'Holy' girl).
C: She is getting a baby as well.

## Games

[Over half of the children mentioned games that they played either in school or at home. The games referred to by the children are listed below.

All the games cited were played at school apart from the games marked with '*'. These games were played exclusively at home.]

| Games Boys Mentioned | Games Girls Mentioned |
|---|---|
| Hurling | Skipping |
| Bulldog | *Skipping stones on river |
| Football | Racing |
| Racing | Running |
| 'Following' | *Knocker gawlai (knocking |
| Running | on doors and running away) |
| 'Fighting' | Hurling |
| Soccer | Cops and robbers |
| Computer games | Hide-and-Seek |

## Travelling

[A very small number of children mentioned the Traveller tradition of moving around during the summer months. Travelling was once central to Traveller culture. The 'boulder policy' by local authorities prohibiting access to traditional sites and lack of official transient halting sites, has reesulted in a significant decline in Traveller mobility.]

I: *Do you like pulling out?*
C: Yeah, 'cause we are going to the Reek (Croagh Patrick).
I: How long are you going, for summer or a few weeks?
C: Two weeks and then we are going on to another place.
I: Do you like travelling? Do you like it better than being in a house?
C: Yeah 'cause I'm bringing Spot (pony) and I can go on her back.
I: When away what do you miss about being in the house?
C: Cleaning the yard.
I: Would you miss school?
C: No, only art.

*I: Do you like staying in one place?*

C: No we don't stay in one place, sometimes we goes travelling.

I: Where would you go off travelling?

C: The last time we went to Donegal, then to Mayo, then to Galway and back.

I: Do you like travelling?

C: Yeah!

I: Do you meet other people when you are travelling?

C: When I meet someone you know like when we are with each other and then we pull away and we meet them again sometime.

**Commentary**

In the main all the children who engaged with the issue of ethnicity had some awareness of the concept of difference. They were aware of the fact that as Travellers they were different from other children. Travellers were viewed to be different because they live in chalets, are treated differently in school, have horses, are 'nicer' than country people and wear earrings. Some children addressed the issue by contrasting themselves to the settled child. In these instances the children responded with answers such as 'country' people don't fight, are better at colouring and painting and don't get punished (at school).

Most of the children used the term 'country' people when talking about the settled community. Two children talked about 'buffers' when referring to the settled community. 'Buffer' is a more derogatory Traveller term for a settled person. One child noted that her friends did not like people who lived in 'caravans'. She, however, did not think there was any difference between Travellers and country people (unless her teacher told her!). This child lives in a caravan herself though she does not allude to it in the interviews. One child described himself as 'settled' because his family did not travel. In a later interview he states that he knew that he was different from 'country' people because country people live in houses and he lives in a chalet.

The interview pictures and sequence cards helped some of the children to talk about ethnicity and difference. One child was shown a picture of three children painting together. The picture consisted of two white girls and one black boy. When the interviewee was asked what he saw he focused on the black boy only. The child states that nobody will play with the black boy, but on further reflection he says that some children would play with him 'if he was fast enough'. From the interviews it is apparent that the skill which gains Traveller boys greatest respect and attention in the school playground is the skill of running or being 'fast'. Having the capacity to run quickly appears to correlate with this Traveller boy's perception of successful participation in the school playground. Whether this implies the ability to run away from the other children in the playground or that the skill enhances their chances of integrating and playing games with the other boys, is not clear. Further exploration of this theme with the child might have ascertained if and in what ways he identified or did not identify with the black child in the picture. In a subsequent interview this child talked about being punished in school for poor behaviour. He linked his punishment to the fact that he was a Traveller. The child's personal experience of discrimination as a Traveller may have heightened his awareness of difference.

Place of residence, form of accommodation, possession of horses and physical appearance were the identifiable features of ethnic difference for the Traveller children in this study. Holding their ethnic identity without experiencing discrimination is extremely difficult for most Travellers. This was confirmed by the Traveller researchers. They revealed that in their own experience many Limerick Travellers frequently conceal their identity or home address in order to avoid discrimination. Some local Traveller mothers divest their school-going children of earrings and jewellery to offset discrimination they may encounter as a result of being physically identified as a Traveller. It was felt that many Traveller children learn strategies early on in their lives and may in time begin to act out of this negative experience.

Some of the children, mainly the boys, in the study tended to compare themselves with or measure themselves against the settled 'country' child. Country children 'paint better', 'they don't fight', they 'think they are cleaner', and 'they don't get punished' (at school) and 'they don't live in caravans'. It would appear that these children have begun to internalise the typical negative stereotyping of Travellers as people who are dirty, who fight and who get into trouble in school. One child, however, appeared to be struggling with the negative perception of Travellers. He stated, with great passion that country people *think* that they are cleaner than Travellers'. This was the only example of a child who showed signs of critiquing or challenging the conventional manner in which society frequently portrays the Traveller community.

Two very different experiences emerge from the children who chatted about their classroom seating arrangements. One child refers to the room in which she receives learning support. The room displays several pictures/posters depicting Traveller culture and lifestyle. Over the course of the interviews it was obvious that the child is comfortable with the room, has made it her own and feels very much at ease in it. At times during the interviews this child voluntarily walked around the room pointing out various items and books with enthusiasm. This child appears very happy with the seating position in this setting. No mention was made of the main classroom seating arrangement.

The other interviewees who talked about this topic present a different picture. In these cases the children, both boys, are talking about the main classroom setting. Both children are seated either at or towards the back of the classroom. The children openly express how they feel about where they are seated. One child seems 'happy' to be at the side of the classroom because he is near the computer. The same child did not eagerly seek to sit near the front of the classroom. This seating arrangement would demand greater attention from and engagement with the class teacher, thus facilitating and challenging the child's participation in classroom interactions. One gets the impression that for this particular child his seating position increases the opportunity for switching out from classroom activity, decreasing teacher awareness of him and thus diminishing the child's chances for active and purposeful learning.

The second boy who chats about where he sits in class offers an insight into a child who is very much aware of the reasons for being seated at the back of the classroom. This child knows that his behaviour towards the other 'young fellows' has resulted in the teacher placing him at the back of the room. While he appears to have some realisation that sitting at the top of the classroom might increase his chances of learning, he is also aware of his tendency to 'talk to people', which may be easier to do at the back of the room!

It is probably fair to say that both these boys find school academically challenging. These are the same children who disclose a sense of social isolation and discrimination in school and portray aggressive behaviour in the playground. Being placed at the back of the class may be the result of their misbehaviour. It may also be due to the class teacher's inability to deal with the children and to engage with them effectively in classroom activities; most likely it is a combination of both. The reasons underlying a Traveller child's poor behaviour or performance in schools needs careful and honest investigation. A heightened awareness and deep understanding of Traveller culture by the class teacher and the school principal should constantly inform and underpin all investigations and evaluations into Traveller education.

Many children showed a high degree of curiosity over the course of the interviews. This curiosity took many forms. Some children checked out the personal background of the interviewers. They expressed curiosity about who the interviewers were, where they lived, who they knew within the Traveller community and who they knew within the school setting. The girls were more likely than the boys to ask personal details about family, children and husbands. Many children, both boys and girls, were interested in the interview process itself. They were curious about factual things such as how many interviews there would be, who was being interviewed, how long the interviews would last. It is a girl who inquires if the same questions were being asked of every child. It would appear that she had checked this out with one of the other girls between interviews! Finally almost all the children showed an interest in the equipment. These children asked what the equipment was for, requested if they could talk into the machines and hear themselves played back at the end of the interview. No child asked who would be listening to the interviews afterwards.

While the Traveller children in this study seemed to be more preoccupied with home-related jobs and tasks than with play, some did talk about the games that they liked to play. A lot of the games talked about were played in school. Fewer games were played at home. Some did, however, talk about games at home. The two boys who live beside a large housing estate where positive interaction between the Traveller and settled child existed were the ones who most frequently talked about playing games. With the exception of computer games, all games cited were of an active and outdoor nature.

Traditionally, Travellers are a nomadic people. Moving from place to place has always been an intrinsic aspect of the Traveller culture. While the children were not asked directly about the tradition of travelling, when it came up the interviewers encouraged them to talk about the experience. The topic came up with a very small number of children. The fact that so few children mentioned the tradition is not surprising. Due to the lack of provision of official transient sites and the restrictions placed on Traveller movement through the local authority 'boulder policy' many young Traveller children have little or no experience of 'travelling'. Given that the other children failed to raise the custom it may indicate a change in the nomadic patterns among Limerick Traveller families.

# Conclusion

## Summary of Findings

Now that we have come to the end of our research and our findings move out into the public arena we trust that some of what we have discovered will find resonance in the hearts and minds of a wider community, especially among those involved in Traveller education and in community development. We hope that the study will provoke a certain kind of awareness, the kind of understanding that leads to creatively exploring and celebrating Traveller children's lives both in and out of the classroom and that allows the Traveller voice to be heard clearly. It is only when we begin to listen carefully to that voice will our education system fully acknowledge and respect the Traveller child's personal and collective history, identity, culture and tradition. To listen actively we must all be prepared to open our minds to seeing the world from new and different perspectives.

This study points towards such perspectives. It offers a window into the imaginings of a small group of Limerick Traveller children. It gives invaluable insights into how they view their life, their passions and their experience of primary school.

The size of the sample prohibits us from applying the data to the general Traveller population. However, we wish to put forward some conclusions that while specific to the Traveller children participating in the research may be useful pointers in future research around Traveller education. A range of themes emerged in the course of the study. Some of these themes recurred time and again. We have singled out ten dominant threads that ran consistently throughout the interviews. They are:

- That family was central to the Traveller children's life.
- That the Traveller children took on responsibilities in the home.
- That school was not talked about enthusiastically by the Traveller children.
- That the school day was perceived by the Traveller children as long and boring.
- That teachers were most liked when they were fair, let the children out to play and did activity related subjects with them.
- That some Traveller boys' relationships with the school principal, in the main, revolved around reprimand and punishment.
- That both the Traveller boys and the Traveller girls talked passionately about horses.
- That the Traveller children were hesitant to explore topics of a personal nature.
- That the school world did not appear to be connected with the Traveller child's world.
- That the Traveller children wished for improved standards of living accommodation.

The themes above have a familiar echo – the link between education and appropriate accommodation for Traveller children, the centrality of family within the Traveller community, the significance of horses, the importance of fairness in relationships with school staff, the failure of the system to meet Traveller children's academic needs, the problem status approach to

Traveller children within the school system, the Traveller child's love of activity and the outdoors. This piece of research is but the tip of the iceberg in terms of understanding and celebrating the Traveller child. More work needs to be undertaken.

Encouraging and training members of the Traveller community to conduct research within their own community opens the way for all kinds of challenging outcomes. When the initiative involves the partnership of a local Traveller Community Development Project and a major education institution the creative possibilities are even greater. This study marks a small but significant beginning. May it offer encouragement to other Travellers and education providers to participate in similar ventures at both local and national levels.

# Recommendations

**That the Traveller researchers of the working group take a lead role in overseeing the implementation of the recommendations emerging from the study and that relevant training and support be sought to facilitate the researchers in this work.**

- That Limerick Travellers Development Group seek funding from the Department of Community, Rural and Gaeltacht Affairs to secure a dedicated education officer to work strategically in ensuring the effective participation of Traveller children in the education system in the Limerick city and its environs.

- That Limerick Travellers Development Group and Mary Immaculate College in conjunction with the Traveller researchers continue to work collaboratively to uncover the root causes that create barriers to local Traveller children's successful experience within the primary education system.

- That Limerick Travellers Development Group in conjunction with the Traveller researchers gather together a core group of relevant local educational personnel to explore new and imaginative ways towards ensuring positive education outcomes for Limerick Traveller children and to lobby for change in this regard.

- That the skills, knowledge and experience of the Traveller researchers acquired through this study be acknowledged locally and nationally and that they be called on to conduct further educational research.

- That Traveller Cultural Awareness Training be delivered to all staff and Boards of Management in Limerick primary schools, that Traveller parents be trained to develop and present such training and that Limerick Travellers

Development Group in conjunction with the Traveller researchers would take the lead in this initiative.

- That Limerick Travellers Development Group in conjunction with the Traveller researchers encourage Traveller parents to become active members of Limerick primary school boards of management.

## Actions Arising

To ensure the successful implementation of the recommendations the following actions have been identified by the working group:

1.  To develop a presentation on the research outcomes and to deliver the same to the Traveller community and to relevant educational bodies in Limerick city.

2.  To set up a meeting with the Co-ordinator of Limerick Travellers Development Group and the President of Mary Immaculate to explore avenues for continued joint research and support initiatives in Traveller education locally.

3.  To seek funding for on-going research into Traveller education at primary level.

# Words to the Wise

Participating in this study has taught us an immense amount about ourselves, about team work and about the research process. We would like to share some of what we have learnt with others who may wish to undertake an endeavour of a similar kind. In offering our 'words of wisdom', born out of our hard earned experience we think particularly of first time Traveller researchers. We hope these simple guidelines may help steer their path and assist them in the avoidance of at least some pitfalls!

## To the First Time Traveller Researcher

- Be courageous – say 'yes' to participating in a research project.
- Be confident – trust that you can do it.
- Be realistic – know that learning something takes time, patience and energy.
- Be true to Traveller culture and traditions – they belong to you.
- Be clear about ground rules with the group – what everyone agrees to can be readily applied.
- Be insistent about the importance of group decision making – it takes time but it builds trust in the group.
- Be eager to acknowledge everybody's experience – everybody's story deserves respect.
- Be committed to teamwork – remember two heads are better than one.
- Be willing to state what you are good at – what is needed is often under our noses.
- Be open to change – change though challenging can also be exciting.
- Be flexible – listen to the individual needs within the group.
- Be committed to the work – it is better when everybody pulls their weight.
- Be honest – openly tell others how you see things.

- Be wise – have a bit of fun as you go along.
- Be loyal to the group – people are more important than the results.
- Be confidential – keep personal issues within the group.
- Be professional at all times – act as you would like others to act towards you.
- Be ready to learn new things about yourself – learning can be exciting.
- Be steadfast – keep going even when the going gets tough.
- Be patient with yourself and with others – everything has a habit of working out in the end.

**To Researchers Considering Interviewing Traveller Children**
- Be sensitive to Traveller culture, customs and values.
- Be aware that family is the heart of Traveller life.
- Be open to learn from the Traveller child.
- Be honest with the child, yourself and the process.
- Be determined to give time to build the relationship with the child.
- Be accepting of the Traveller community's sense of privacy.
- Be ready to share some personal information with the child.
- Be eager to stay with the truth of what you hear.
- Be spontaneous and relaxed.
- Be non-judgmental.
- Be prepared.
- Be confidential at all times.
- Be an active listener.
- Be affirming and positive with the child.
- Be true to yourself, putting on an act rarely fools a child.
- Be alert, focus on what the child is and is not saying.
- Be at the interview venue a half an hour before the interview session.
- Be familiar in the use of the equipment.
- Be professional.
- Be prepared to have fun and to enjoy the experience.

**To those considering a collaborative research initiative**
Collaborative research is always challenging. It demands an honest and open meeting of minds, traditions, values, philosophies and methodologies. We thought that it might be helpful to list some things that we felt were worth bearing in mind if you were considering embarking on a collaborative partnership based research project.

- Collaborative research moves to a particular rhythm and takes time, patience and practice.
- Different perspectives bring different world views, visions and values. These need to be identified, validated and worked with creatively and honestly.
- Family and child-care issues will emerge for many.
- Respect the context of people's lives. We are all constantly effected by what is happening within and around us.
- Adopting new working styles is not easy. Collaborative research cannot work unless people are prepared to explore different work practices and methods.
- Everyone needs to be prepared to have their perspective challenged.
- Identifying similarities can help in working creatively with difference.
- Consultation and agreement are pivotal elements to collaborative research.
- Establishing trust is a central component to any partnership endeavour. Trust is often earned and takes time, energy and a nurturing environment.
- Define roles clearly and keep the division of labour fair and equal.
- Recognise and challenge discrimination when it arises. Sometimes it takes others to show up what we are blind to in ourselves.
- Encourage collective responsibility for the whole process. This takes time but the quality of the process is greater in the end.
- Safeguard the relationships within the group.

- Create a safe place where each person's culture and tradition is honoured.
- Acknowledge the barriers to participation. What constitutes a benefit for you may be a barrier for someone else.
- Allow plenty of time for the initiative to be completed. True collaborative work cannot be rushed. It demands generous degrees of time and space.
- Seek ongoing evaluative and facilitative help. It is good to have an 'outsider' comment on what is happening.
- Be alert to the balance of power. Sometimes in the interest of getting things done a few people can unwittingly 'take over'.
- Empower people to take ownership of the work.
- Celebrate the achievements along the way. It is not always necessary to wait for the finale!